CHANGING WORLD/CHANGING TEACHERS

CHANGING WORLD/CHANGING TEACHERS

OWEN A. HAGEN

Chairman, Department of Elementary Education
St. Cloud State College
St. Cloud, Minnesota

GOODYEAR PUBLISHING COMPANY, INC.
PACIFIC PALISADES, CALIFORNIA

Current printing (last digit):
10 9 8 7 6 5 4 3 2 1

ISBN: 0-87620-178-8 (paper)
        0-87620-179-6 (cloth)

Library of Congress Catalog Card Number: 72-87169
        Y-1788-2 (paper)
        Y-1796-5 (cloth)

Printed in the United States of America

ACKNOWLEDGEMENTS

To expose one's concept of teachers and teaching in a time when there is world emphasis on education seems a somewhat overwhelming, perhaps risky, and most certainly challenging undertaking. It is only now, as I look back over the work, that I fully realize how great a task it really was and how grateful I must be to the many people who made it possible.

First, I owe so much to my wife Norma, for her constant encouragement and help in the development of the book, and to my children Robert, Kristine, Kari, and John whose patience and understanding were called for, and freely given, on so many occasions. My mother Anna Hagen also deserves a special acknowledgement for her encouragement throughout my teaching career.

Special mention must also be given to Dr. Dorothy Skeel, Dr. John Michaelis, and James P. Levy for their critical appraisal of the manuscript throughout its development. Thanks also to Jim van Maanen, Josephine Austin, David Grady, Sue MacLaurin and all others responsible for the preparation of the manuscript and the production of the book.

For the perceptive artist's drawings throughout the book, I must thank my close friend, William Ellingson, whose rich outlook on life, living, and education, together with his rare artistic ability helped me translate many important thoughts in a visual manner.

Finally, I must offer my gratitude to Dr. Alice Miel, Dr. Arthur Foshay, Dr. Florence Stratemeyer, Dr. Leland Jacobs, Dr. Gordon McKenzie, Dr. John Jarolimek, Monica DuCharme and the hundreds of students with whom I had the opportunity to work and who have contributed so richly to my constantly changing concept of teacher.

ARTIST'S DRAWINGS

The artist's sketches throughout the book were created by William Ellingson, art professor at St. Cloud State College, St. Cloud, Minnesota.

PHOTOGRAPHS

The photographs in the book are offered through the courtesy of the Television Studio, School of Education, St. Cloud State College, St. Cloud, Minnesota. Fred Polesak, Director.

CONTENTS

SECTION 2 Multiple Dimensions of Classroom Teaching

SECTION 3   Potpourri

x

INTRODUCTION

CHANGING WORLD/CHANGING TEACHERS is aimed at presenting a
realistic concept of today's classroom teacher in the midst of a rapidly changing world. Even though qualities such as genuineness, understanding, patience,
scholarship and knowledge of the learner are time honored with respect to
desirable characteristics of teachers, there appears to be a need to examine
these qualities and characteristics as they relate to the knowledge explosion,
technological developments in and out of the classroom, shifting value systems in the family, and a host of other changing dimensions of the world in
which we live.

A subtitle of the analysis might well have been "One Concept
of Teacher" for it is surely that and nothing more. Even though the concept of
teacher shared on the following pages is drawn from a wide variety of situations and experiences involving many people, it can still be shared only as one
individual's frame of reference. There are many concepts of teacher which
need to be respected even if strong disagreements in theory and practice exist
and the goal of this analysis is to share one concept with you as you go about
the most important task of all: developing and modifying your own concept
of teacher.

It is in this final sense that CHANGING WORLD/CHANGING
TEACHERS is offered for your examination. The only goal is to stimulate
you, as a person considering teaching or as an experienced teacher in the field,
to question critically and to analyze your own personal concept of teacher.
You cannot take on my concept, or anyone else's for that matter, so I offer it
not as a model but rather as a series of ideas about teachers and teaching for
you to react to and internalize as your personal style and needs dictate. My
emphasis on ideas will, hopefully, explain why I have deliberately chosen to
raise many questions for you to work with and think about, rather than to
pretend to have the answers for you, a liberty exercised by many. Some will
be uncomfortable with this style because they feel a book's major purpose is

to share through the printed word new information and knowledge. Although I respect this position, I would find it extremely narrow if it were the only view possible. Indeed, books may serve many functions and purposes and one I regard to be among the most important is to stimulate further thought. Toward this end, then, CHANGING WORLD/CHANGING TEACHERS is directed.

Perhaps the following excerpt from *Through the Looking-Glass* provides the best analogy for the reading experiences that lie ahead in this book:

> "I should see the garden far better," said Alice to herself, "if I could get to the top of that hill: and here is a path that leads straight to it, at least, no, it doesn't do that, but I suppose it will at last. But how curiously it twists! It's more like a corkscrew than a path!"[1]

Indeed, developing and constantly modifying an operational concept of teacher is a most challenging task and the path does "twist like a corkscrew." There is, of course, no one "path that leads straight to it" and although we are tempted to seek out such a path from time to time we quickly realize the futility of such a goal. CHANGING WORLD/CHANGING TEACHERS is clearly not a single path to "the top of the hill" but it is hoped that the experiences encountered in this modest effort will assist you on your journey and that "your view of the garden" will be improved as a result.

1. Lewis Carroll, *Through the Looking-Glass, and What Alice Found There*, as published originally (London: Macmillan and Co., 1890), p. 26.

To my wife Norma and children:
Rob, Kristi, Kari, and John

TIME, FEBRUARY

along with Thoreau last week—or rather part of the way. Quoting Thoreau's ringing challenge to the state, the signers* announced in full-page ads in the New York Post and the *New York Review of Books* that "1) None of us voluntarily will pay the proposed 10% income tax surcharge or any underigated tax increase. 2) Many of us will not pay that 23% of our current income tax which is being used to finance the war in Viet Nam."

That is not exactly the stuff of which martyrs are made. Chances of the tax surcharge being enacted are still doubtful. Even one one-third of the signers who refuse to pay present taxes are not likely to go to jail. Some of them haven't paid taxes for years on grounds of pacifism. Since they have reported their income and paid part of their tax, the Internal Revenue Service does not take them to court. It attaches their bank accounts or other assets to recover the cost of the tax, plus a penalty of 6% a year. With this in mind, some pacifists keep enough cash in their checking accounts to save themselves and the IRS a lot of trouble.

Eight newspapers felt that the ad advocated violation of U.S. law and refused to carry it. One of the papers to turn it down was the New York Times —much to the chagrin of the ten signers who work for the paper.

SCHOOLS

More Life, Less Trade

U.S. journalism schools are im... ing these days because they a... ing less journalism. At both ... and undergraduate levels, ... are stressing the liberal art... playing the techniques of ... most undergraduate school... of the course requirements ... al journalism, and that ... decreasing even further at s... "The four years of college," ... ert Beyers of Stanford U... such a short time to ac... tion that it should no... learning skills which ... quired outside the cla...

Under Deans I. ... P. Jacobi, Northwe... of Journalism now ... uate students to t... the reporting of p... are offered in ur... tion, science and ... dent who took ... legal system gr... like an adva... course." The sch... just what it is su...

Context of S... too ivory towe... western gives ... perience cover...

* Among the qu...
James Baldwin, ...
Paul Goodman, ...
donald, Henry ...
min Spock, Will...

cago's American. Similarly, some 15 students each quarter go to Washington, where they work out of the National Press Building under the supervision of a professor in residence. The Missouri School of Journalism plans next fall to start sending students to Brussels for a semester, where they will report on EEC, Euratom and other European affairs.

As journalism schools have expanded, they have grown uneasy with even the name journalism. Many now call themselves schools of "communications"... try to deal with the broad ... human dialogue. Stanford ... of Communication, for ... added courses called "C... the Mass Media" and ... Mass Media" to stim... thinking about their wo... content of society. At t... Stanford encourages nonjo... dents to take these course... ing down even more th... ween journalism student... of other disciplines.

As they have received ... er education, many jo... now set their sights ... fields. Enrollment ... journalism school ... bled over the past ... yet a declining pe... go into journalism... year. Careers in bus... public relations or a...

SECTION ONE

The Changing World of Classroom Teaching

The major purpose of Section One is to stimulate thinking and raise questions about the concept of teacher for the 70s and beyond. The world of classroom teaching is dynamic and rapidly changing; many critical issues surround today's classroom teacher. The intent of the discussions that follow is to provoke further and more detailed scholarship in students and teachers who have already chosen teaching as a vocation and for those who are considering entering the profession.

Chapter 1 "The Teacher: Why?" raises questions and issues such as: Who are teachers? Why do we need them? What do they do? What qualities should they possess? Why do people choose teaching as a career? Chapter 2 exposes many of the myths that surround the role of teacher and illustrates why these ideas are outdated.

The learner's perspective of classroom teachers is shared in Chapter 3 as nursery school through graduate school learners honestly and openly share their concepts of teacher. Chapter 4 is aimed at nonverbal communication; through a series of photographs and sketches, the reader is taken from the early days to the contemporary 70s.

The final chapter explores the major changes in American education and the new demands placed on teachers as a result of these changes. New dimensions in the teachers' role for the future are identified with the intent of exploring these dimensions in greater detail in Section Two.

The most important consideration, of course, is your personal relationship to the changing teaching world. Hopefully, your frame of reference will be the base for the questions raised in Section One.

THE
TEACHER:
Why?

Teaching means "to instruct." Personally, I am not much interested in instructing another in what he should know or think. "To impart knowledge or skill." My reaction is, why not be more efficient, using a book or programmed learning? "To make to know." Here my hackles rise. I have no wish to make anyone know something. "To show, guide, direct." As I see it, too many people have been shown, guided, directed. So I come to the conclusion that I do mean what I said. Teaching is, for me a relatively unimportant and vastly overvalued activity.[1]

1. Carl R. Rogers, *Freedom To Learn* (Columbus, Ohio: Charles E. Merrill, 1969), p. 103.

How would you describe the teacher in this photograph? From a physical standpoint it doesn't appear to be too difficult—six feet tall, 175 pounds, dark hair, medium build, neat appearance, and so on. One might even comment about the smile and speculate about personality and mood. Because of the physical contact illustrated in the photograph, one might reflect on this teacher's relationship with students, but that would be stretching things without really knowing, wouldn't it? Actually, the photograph provides us with very little information about this teacher; in fact, if I had not told you he was a teacher, is there anything in the photograph that makes you assume he is?

The photograph doesn't tell us, for example, anything about this teacher's basic commitment to the teaching profession. It doesn't tell us anything about his genuineness in working with children; about his understanding of how children grow and develop; about his teaching style and the rationale behind it; about his ability to make critical decisions relating to other human beings; or about a host of other such traits and characteristics.

Words, as well as photographs, can sometimes fall short of providing adequate information about certain questions. Take the general question, what is a teacher? Webster's Dictionary states that a teacher is "one who teaches, or instructs; esp., one whose occupation is to instruct; an instructor."[2] Consider the phrases "to instruct," "to input knowledge," "to make known," and "to guide" found in the quote from Carl Rogers which led us into this chapter. What do these phrases tell you about a teacher? What don't they tell you?

2. *Webster's New Collegiate Dictionary* (Springfield, Mass.: G. & C. Merriam, 1953), p. 871.

What about statements like Teachers are generally oriented toward middle-class ideas and they aspire to service-related activity or Teachers by nature are quite conservative or Teachers are people who work with their heads, not their hands? Do these statements tend to classify teachers to the point of obscuring uniquenesses that exist? Do many people hold a general, stereotyped image of what a teacher is? What about the following example?

Five young men had just completed putting in the foundation supports for a swimming pool in a large suburban back yard when the lady of the house asked if they would like a refreshment break. The summer heat motivated a prompt, positive reply and soon the five men were seated beneath a shade tree, drinking beer and lemonade. After refilling their glasses, their hostess remarked, "Your business must really take a nose dive during the winter months."

"Not ours, Ma'am," replied one of the workers. "We just work for Landy Construction Company during the summers. All of us teach during the school year."

The housewife's almost involuntary comment reflected her apparent shock, "My goodness, I would never have guessed that you were teachers."

Why should this intelligent lady have been surprised that these young men were teachers? Was it the way they looked or talked or acted? Was it the dirt on their hands and faces? Was it the beer that four of the men drank? Is working at a summer construction job too menial a job to be filled by college-educated men?

Very possibly, the lady herself would experience difficulty in explaining her surprise. Like many adults, she has certain expectations about what a teacher is; these men, in their roles as laborers, did not fit those expectations. Similarly, had the men said they were lawyers, airline pilots, garbage collectors, or accountants, she would have been equally unable to explain her surprise. One of the traits of that most intelligent of animals—the human being—is his propensity to classify; but too often the uninformed person, or the one who seldom questions the stereotypes, permits the similarities within one category to obscure the differences. In the category of teachers, these differences are simply too important to ignore or gloss over.

To explore the differences, to examine not only what a teacher is, but also what he is not, we might well begin with a series of very basic questions: What motivates people to want to become teachers—service, money, prestige, challenge, not knowing what else to do, love of education, desire to change education, or wanting to work with young people? What type of background and professional training do teachers need? What characteristics are deemed desirable for success in classroom teaching? What makes teachers want to leave the profession once they have entered it?

These questions represent only an initial sampling of the type of questions that might be generated when exploring the nature and role of a classroom teacher. Other more penetrating questions emerge from an examination of actual teacher behavior.

Dedication

For example, consider Janet Loretto, an elementary teacher in a small midwestern rural community. Janet has taught the third grade in this school district for the past fourteen years, has a B.S. degree from a nearby state college, and is regarded by her colleagues and community as an above average classroom teacher. Consumed by her work, Janet spends large amounts of her time at school and in her classroom. It is not at all unusual to find her arriving at school at 7:00 A.M. and leaving the school at 5:30 P.M., only to return shortly after 7:00 P.M. to complete her planning for the next day. There are those who say that all teachers should have this kind of dedication. Do you agree? Should classroom teachers generally be expected to reflect their devotion to teaching through such time commitments? Should classroom teachers be expected to work extra hours or to take on extracurricular activities (if indeed there is something that can be labeled "extracurricular") without being compensated financially for time spent in such areas? What type of time demands are a part of the role of a teacher? Do time demands extend beyond the bells that start and end the school day?

What about Guy Peterson, a high-school English teacher, town councilman, church board member, local Democratic party leader, and news commentator for the local radio station? Guy doesn't arrive at school at 7:00 A.M., nor is he ever seen around the school later on in the afternoon or evening unless it's for a meeting. Guy is also regarded as an above average teacher by his colleagues and community and he appears in every way to be performing adequately in his English classroom. How does such varied and active participation in local community and political activities relate to Guy Peterson's role as a classroom teacher?

Should teachers assume neutral positions on controversial subjects and issues? Should teachers assume additional responsibilities beyond classroom teaching for which they are paid? Should school policy dictate whether a teacher can be seen in a local tavern, the type of organizations to which he belongs, or his general behavior and activity outside of school time?

Emotional Stability

What type of emotional and mental stability is desirable for a classroom teacher? Are teachers of a certain temperament? Should they be? Are there certain pressures and demands placed on today's classroom teachers that makes their emotional stability an even more important factor than in other professions? What types of feelings, for example, are generated by the following incident involving James Murray, a first-year junior-high-school math teacher? James has just passed three of his students in the hall, and he overhears one of them saying, "You aren't kidding, Mr. Murray's classes are really a drag. None of the kids like him. . ." Are there certain qualities that teachers should possess to assist them in dealing with student, parent, colleague, and administrative constructive and nonconstructive evaluatory comments, whether they are justified or unjustified? What things should a teacher have going for him to deal with a more serious attack on self such as, "You're only a lousy teacher and you can't make me do anything. Go to hell." Should teachers get angry? Should teachers feel comfortable about letting any of their emotions be exposed to their students? Are remarks like those overheard by James Murray only directed at poor teachers? What distinguishes a poor teacher from a good or excellent teacher?

Rewards

What are the major rewards for teachers? Is there a sense of reward that comes from direct verbal and nonverbal reactions of students and fellow workers? Does this vary from nursery-school teachers to teachers in graduate programs? What kind of reward, for example, is felt in situations implied by these remarks? "Hey, Mr. Jacobson, I've got it!" or "I need your help, Miss Olson, I just can't seem to get the hang of this," or "Now I see what you mean. Say, this really isn't so hard after all." Do these statements provide some reward for teachers, or does it require more direct, positive human reaction, like: "You're the greatest teacher I have ever had!" or "Mr. Benson, John wouldn't miss a day of school this year. He is as excited about school as I have ever seen him. You are really doing a fine job with your class."?

To raise further questions about this dimension of the concept of teacher, we might look at Barbara Rogers, a middle-school teacher in an inner-city area. Here she comes, floating down the hall as though she were ten feet tall. The smile on her face and tears in her eyes would tell anyone who meets her that *it's great to be a teacher*! Barbara's exhilaration was brought about by an experience she had had five minutes earlier with one of her thirteen-year-old students. Carla, a student from a home with economic, marital, and other problems, who assumes too much responsibility for her age, had stopped Mrs. Rogers in the hall, grabbed her hand, and with a rare smile on her face stated in excited fashion: "Oh, Mrs. Rogers, I bet you can't guess what I am going to do tonight. *My dad and I* are going to the show, and then we are going to the diner. Isn't that great? Do you remember when we were talking the other day about people's feelings and stuff, and I told you after class that this was fine for some people but not for me because nobody cared about my feelings anyway? Well, I was wrong. My dad really cares. I was telling him about the things we talked about in class, like how sometimes people really care more than they show you. He said, 'that's true,' and we talked for a long time about it. He even had tears in his eyes sometimes. Gee, he must really care, eh?"

How Involved?

How personal is classroom teaching and the role of the teacher? How involved does a teacher become in the personal life of his students? How involved should a teacher get? Patricia Crawford, a third-year, sixth-grade teacher in a large metropolitan community, has a girl in her class who comes to school in clothes that are both dirty and in dire need of mending. Is this problem one that Patricia should get involved with? How do teachers work with homes and/or welfare agencies on problems like these and others? Should they? What role does a teacher assume in the case of a student whose mother has died, in the case of a child who appears "to have everything," in the case of a student with personal problems related to drugs or alcohol, in the case of an unwed pregnant girl? Are these things really part of the world of a teacher?

Ethics

Imagine that you are seated in a faculty lounge of a large elementary school with a number of other teachers, and you hear this conversation: "Boy, that Jimmy Wilson is driving me up a tree. I just don't know what to do about him. He is always into something, and he just can't seem to settle down. Of course, he has the free run of his home, and that mother of his is his biggest problem. If she would only spend more time at home, he probably wouldn't have so many problems." Or suppose you hear a comment about the building principal (not in the lounge at the time), "I see where Old Ironsides has called another meeting for Thursday afternoon. I suppose we are going to sit around for another hour and listen to him make all his announcements again." What about talking about other people? Do teachers really ever make such remarks? Should they? What type of ethical behavior should be expected of a professional classroom teacher? Should teachers ever talk about students, parents, fellow teachers, and administrators in settings other than those that have a direct bearing and relationship to the teacher's professional role? When would it be appropriate? What type of personal temptations must teachers guard against in remaining ethical when working with such a wide range of individuals?

Professional Training

What type of professional training is needed for today's teacher? To probe this area a bit deeper, consider the following examples of two junior-high-school science teachers.

It was a great day for Ernie Cline when he received his B.S. in education and the teaching certificate which accompanied it. Ever since his high-school days when he had worked as a nature studies instructor at a youth camp, Ernie had wanted to teach junior-high-school science. But, gad! getting there was a drag! His science courses at the university had been tolerable and a few of them really pretty good. But most of the other stuff was so much rot, just one requirement after another that Ernie had put up with because he wanted his sheepskin.

But three years ago Ernie made it, and now he teaches science to seventh and eighth graders. He's generally regarded by his students and colleagues as a good teacher, one who stimulates students to learn and is able to offer them assistance in that learning. And Ernie himself continues to learn —but certainly not by taking courses or reading textbooks or any of that kind of stuff. He put that stuff behind him when he graduated, Ernie thinks, and he's not about to go through it again. Let the others get master's degrees if they want them, but not Ernie. He just wants to teach. He can learn enough from watching his students and from thinking about his work. Not for him, the life of Proxmire.

The Jeff Proxmire that Ernie compares himself with is just down the hall, another science teacher in Ernie's department. In many aspects of their training, Jeff and Ernie are alike: both went to state universities, both majored in science education, both took essentially the same required courses. But their similarities in training end there. Jeff spent each summer going to college, working in the bookstore to pay his costs. He studied in the summers because he wanted to take more courses, "To learn more at the best place there is to learn it" is the way he puts it. When he graduated, Jeff had 37 more credits than were required. To Jeff, college courses were fun, even the required courses in economics or western civilization or freshmen composition.

And even now Jeff continues to take courses. He began teaching with Ernie three years ago and already has earned a master's degree, an achievement made possible by his regularly driving 60 miles two nights a week to the nearest university for part-time courses and going there every summer for full-time work. He has just recently completed his university application for work on a doctorate. He says that he doubts that he'll ever complete that degree, but he does want to continue to take courses, and the university requires that he be enrolled in some program. So far, Jeff's own role as a student has not hindered his working with his own students. They like his classes and feel that they profit from them. Like Ernie, he is a good teacher.

These descriptions of Ernie and Jeff raise some questions. For example, How much education should a teacher have before he begins teaching? How much of this work should be in subject matter courses and how much in education courses that concentrate on the pedagogical aspect of teaching? Once certified, should a teacher be expected to continue taking formal courses? If so, how often and of what kind? Who pays for the cost of such courses? Do you think a teacher with more education will be a better teacher than one whose education has stopped at the baccalaureate level? Suppose you ran a school system, would you pay teachers according to the amount of education they have? (This is one of the two most common bases for determining teacher salaries, the other being teacher experience.)

Pressures

What about pressures concomitant with the role of a teacher? Do they exist? If so, in what shape and form? Does the teacher directly feel pressure from the community with respect to his program and behavior in the classroom? What types of administrative pressures and pressures from colleagues are part of classroom teaching? What about deadlines and maintaining minimum levels of teaching performance as evaluated by others?

Does teaching amid immense technological and social change add pressures to the teacher's role? Does the constant need for more advanced training, and the attempt to keep abreast of the rapid changes in his field, put too much pressure on the classroom teachers? Are there pressures to write, to conduct research, and to innovate? What type of student-created pressures exist? Are there economic pressures attached to being a teacher? Do new organizational patterns create new sources of pressure for teachers, such as team organization and nongrading, etc.? Perhaps the most fundamental concern of all might be raised by thinking about a teacher standing in front of a group of children on the first day of school. Indeed, what types of pressures and concerns are related to the fact that this teacher is about to assume a major leadership responsibility in working with these children for long periods of time? How would you feel in a similar position?

Take the position of Carl Nellermoe, social-studies teacher and chairman of the local salary committee. Carl had recently presented the teachers' salary recommendations to the board of education and, in the middle of that presentation, one of the board members stopped him and said, "I have had about enough of this; teachers' salaries are already too high, and there are plenty of people in this community who agree with me. You will have to prove to us that you deserve an increase just as we have to do in our jobs." How does Carl respond as a representative of the other teachers in the district? Do you suppose he feels pressure in this situation? How would you feel under similar circumstances?

Intellect

Susan Marshall is a senior in high school and wants to become a teacher. According to her teachers, she always has. One of her science teachers was commenting just the other day about Susan's desire to become a teacher and on her potential for that role. "Susan will make a fine teacher. She has a straight A average in high school and will graduate at the top of her class." What about intellectual power and the role of a teacher? In what way is intellect basic to success in classroom teaching? Does it vary according to the level at which one works? How much does a teacher need to know before he assumes the teaching role in any given situation? Is there any truth to the statement, "I can teach most any subject even if I haven't had a lot of background in the area. I can work with my students, learn with them, motivate them, guide them, direct them and so on, even if I don't know all the information basic to an area beforehand. That's more what a teacher should be doing anyway." Do you agree?

Decision Making

What about the role of a classroom teacher as a decision maker?, For what types of decisions are teachers responsible? Do classroom teachers, for example, make decisions about the nature and structure of the curriculum for their classrooms, schools, or school districts? Do they make decisions about the school budget? If no, should they? Do teachers participate in making decisions about personnel who are hired in their school or system? Are teachers responsible for making decisions about such things as teacher load, the student makeup of the classes they teach, workshop agendas, welfare concerns, and a host of other such matters? Are teachers making more decisions than they have in the past? Is the nature of these decisions changing? What type of decisions will teachers of the future be expected to make?

What are the major reasons why teachers leave the profession? Why is Timothy Glade, a 25-year-old social-science teacher, a dropout from the teaching ranks? You can almost hear him talking to himself as he packs the last items from his desk on his last day of school. "I'm sure glad that it's all over. I pity the poor fellow who will be taking my place. . ." Was it a problem of relating with students, a problem with the administration, or with his colleagues? Was it lack of support for teaching something he felt was important? Was it an economic reason or a lack of challenge or too much challenge? Could it have something to do with lack of time to perform his required duties, and does this vary from a nursery-school teacher to a college teacher? Was teaching too constricting for Timothy Glade, and did he feel that there were too many restrictions placed on him? Indeed, what are the major problems that contribute to teacher frustrations and concerns, sometimes to the point that teachers leave the profession? Are new problems and concerns being generated, or are the problems the same as for past generations of teachers?

As may be obvious at this point, raising questions about the concept of teacher is a free flowing and basically endless activity. Why do people choose to become teachers? Why a math teacher and not an English teacher? Why an elementary teacher and not a senior-high teacher? What type of teachers will be called for in the future? What are the major problems and rewards that lie ahead? Yes, it is not at all difficult to raise questions about teachers and teaching. Hopefully, however, at this point the question-raising activity will be shifted to you the reader, as I, the author, begin to explore in greater depth my concept of the changing teacher for your reaction, reflection, and of course questioning.

QUESTIONS FOR ANALYSIS

1. Why are you considering teaching as a career or why have you chosen this profession?

2. Do you feel that some individuals have chosen teaching as a career for reasons that you consider questionable? What are these reasons?

3. Do you agree with Carl Rogers that teaching is relatively unimportant and a vastly overvalued activity? Evaluate Rogers' statement.

4. Describe the most outstanding teacher you have had in the past; the least impressive.

5. What experiences have you had which illustrate the fact that some individuals stereotype teachers?

6. What is your concept of a dedicated teacher?

7. Describe your own personality characteristics that will be, or are, advantages and those that are disadvantages to you in teaching.

8. To what extent should a tight marketplace influence the decision to become a teacher?

SELECTED REFERENCES

13

"The Beginning Teacher." *Bulletin of the National Association of Secondary School Principals* 330 (October 1968).

Henderson, George, and Bibens, Robert F. *Teachers Should Care: Social Perspectives of Teaching.* New York: Harper & Row, Publishers, 1970.

Hyman, Ronald. T. *Ways of Teaching.* Philadelphia: J. B. Lippincott Company, 1970.

Jackson, Philip W. *Life in Classrooms.* New York: Holt, Rinehart and Winston, 1968.

Jersild, Arthur T. *When Teachers Face Themselves.* New York: Teachers College, Columbia University, 1955.

Morrison, A., and McIntyre, D. *Teachers and Teaching.* Baltimore, Maryland: Penguin, 1969.

Ohles, John F. *Introduction to Teaching.* New York: Random House, 1970.

Rogers, Carl R. *Freedom to Learn.* Columbus, Ohio: Charles E. Merrill, 1969.

Ryan, Kevin, and Cooper, James M. *Those Who Can, Teach.* Boston: Houghton Mifflin, 1972.

Shumsky, Abraham. *In Search of Teaching Style.* New York: Appleton-Century Crofts, 1968.

Silberman, Charles E. *Crisis In The Classroom.* New York: Random House, 1970.

14

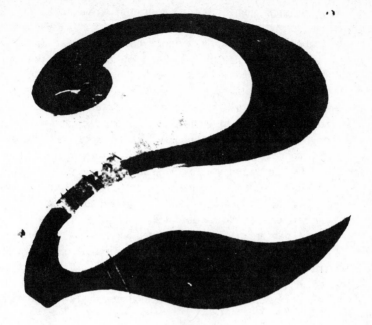

THE
TEACHER:
An Outdated Perspective

*The demands made by a rapidly changing and increasingly complex
society have radically altered the teacher's role and the conditions
under which that role is carried out. The prospective teacher
finds that the concept of teaching he formed as a student, and
sometimes even the concept of teaching that informs his professional
training, is either obsolescent or obsolete.*[1]

1. Robert H. Anderson, *Teaching in a World of Change* (New
York: Harcourt Brace Jovanovich, 1966), p. 3.

The used car salesman opened the front door of a four-year-old automobile and continued in rhythm with his sales pitch, "Yes, it's a very clean car and in tip-top shape. It was owned by a schoolteacher and she was the only owner of the car. . . ." Why is it that this salesman would comment on the fact that a schoolteacher had owned the car previously? Does he always indicate professional or work background of previous owners—"a druggist owned this car," "the owner of the Five Star Bar owned this car," "a lawyer owned this car," etc.? Perhaps he does, but I am inclined to think that the salesman felt that his mentioning that this car was owned by a schoolteacher had some sales value: "teachers drive slowly"; "teachers only drive back and forth from their homes to school and maybe to a local college during the summer." Are these assumptions correct? At one period of time, perhaps—yes, to a certain extent (and even this is open to question), but as related to today's classroom teacher—the perspective is clearly outdated.

There are many other outdated perspectives and myths about the teacher. Identification of these myths and illustrations of their remoteness from reality will be the first step in attempting to sort out the crucial elements which relate to today's classroom teacher. In short, we will examine first what a teacher is not before exploring in greater depth what a teacher is or should be.

A Storehouse of Knowledge

The first myth in need of attention might be drawn from a fifth grader's definition of a teacher: "A teacher is someone who is supposed to know everything so he can teach you about it." Even though this sincere definition has both appeal and popularity, it is obvious that nobody would be eligible for teaching if "knowing everything" was among the requirements. This myth is believed by those who feel that a teacher is basically a storehouse of knowledge. The extent to which one has knowledge about a given subject or combination of subjects is the best indicator of his readiness to teach in those fields. The major function of the teacher, as viewed by such individuals, is that of disseminating information and the primary goal of teacher education is to "fill up the storehouse" for the later dissemination.

What has just been said should in no way indicate that the academic knowledge a teacher has is unimportant. On the contrary, it is very important and will be explored in greater depth later in this analysis. The myth exists in the beliefs of many people, including some teachers, that the sharing of knowledge is the only function of a classroom teacher. As we shall see, such sharing is hardly the only function and may, indeed, not even be the most important one.

Knowledge sharing is, of course, part of the work of a classroom teacher and he should have a command of the knowledge that needs to be imparted in certain educational situations; it is more important however, that the teacher be viewed as "an active scholar of his field or fields. In

particular, he must have control of the so called process goals that enable students to acquire, interpret, evaluate, and communicate knowledge."[2] With our knowledge banks growing by leaps and bounds, a teacher really has no other choice.

The Pedestal Teacher

A second myth frequently held about the teacher is that he is basically a model of all good and right and should not illustrate anything other than positive behavior in and out of the classroom. Teachers shouldn't make mistakes.

Again, the intentions which underlie this myth are good ones;

2. Anderson, op. cit., p. 16.

the reality of today's classroom, however, suggests that "myth" is indeed the appropriate term. Teachers do make mistakes.

Teachers are living models, which many educators feel to be the most powerful aspect of teaching, but all modeling is not of a positive nature. A teacher is first of all a human being subjected to the full range of temptations, motivations, needs, and drives that cause him to behave in many different ways, good and bad, the same as all human beings. Some teachers do get angry. Some teachers do distrust, dislike, and suspect. Some teachers are prejudiced in one way or another. Some lack patience and tolerance. There are teachers who are greedy and are consumed by goals of acquiring wordly goods. There are teachers who use deception as a behavioral tool in working with children and youth. There are also teachers who use their professional position to support their personal feelings that they are superior to others. Some teachers are fearful of certain things physical and abstract. Some are quite religious, some are not. Some teachers are nervous and excitable. Some teachers cry and become confused.

The fact is, the deeper you probe into personal and professional dimensions of the thousands of classroom teachers who exist across the country, the wider the range of human behavior good and bad you discover.

Taking drugs, shoplifting, evading income taxes, and even cheating on golf scores, all do turn up in the lives of some teachers as they do for every other human segment of our society.

Consider Wilma Johnson, for example, a senior-high-school speech teacher in a large suburban school system. If you had been in her classroom last evening right after school, you would have overheard her commenting to a teaching colleague, "I am going to call in sick tonight so I will be able to get away a day early for the big ski weekend up at Lookout Mountain, it's really going to be some affair." Then you would have heard her say in a call to the building principal later that evening, "I'm not really sure what it is. Probably just a virus, but I think I will try to check it before it really gets going. . ." To see still another dimension, turn the clock back 48 hours and hear Miss Johnson make these remarks to one of her students who had missed two of her classes in the last week and a half: "Tom, you know you have a responsibility for being in class and your reasons for being absent are just not excusable. . . ."

Yes, teachers are human. Whereas I can state forthrightly that I am proud and honored to be a teacher and further that in general the teaching ranks are made up of a very high-quality level of individuals both from a personal and professional standpoint, I do feel the mask of infallibility must be dropped if we are to expose a realistic and honest image of teachers today. Whereas our goal should be to reduce modeling of undesirable behavior on the part of classroom teachers, to pretend that this behavior doesn't exist is misleading for those who are considering careers in teaching and, for those who are already in the profession, it is dishonest. Theoretically we are working toward improved standards of excellence in the teaching ranks. The problem must be met squarely.

It should be pointed out that certain teachers' weaknesses, when properly exposed to students, can even result in some excellent learning experiences. For example, a teacher who has a fear of height has the opportunity to admit that fear to his students and to share his approach and feelings about dealing with the problem. If properly done, such an admission on the part of a teacher might just be the necessary motivation for a child in his class to expose a fear he has and, hopefully, the communication between child and teacher opens up ways to explore his feelings and ways to deal with them.

Other examples might be offered by looking at teachers who have overcome such problems as drugs, alcohol, extreme poverty, physical handicaps, being dishonest, etc. In any of these instances, the teacher has the opportunity to share at least some facets of his or her personal confrontation with the problem, when appropriate to relevant topics being explored in school. Such personalization should have as its primary purpose and thrust the educational enrichment of a given problem or topic under study and under no circumstances should be used indiscriminately. All teachers should be prepared to "share some cracks in their own humanity" (and we all have them) in order for students to do likewise. To expect students to live in an educational world where only their weaknesses are exposed is unfair and unrealistic. But more on this matter in Chapter Six where we explore the questions of potential loss of respect, parent pressures, and other related issues.

Superiority of Teachers at Higher Levels

Another myth about teachers is the belief that it is more difficult to teach at the college than at the high-school level, at the high-school than at the junior-high level, and at the junior-high than at the elementary or nursery-school levels. This myth is extended somewhat by suggesting that the higher the level you teach, the more significant the contribution you make. Paradoxically, many believe just the reverse—namely, because the most formative years are the early years, the most significant group of educators are those attached to early childhood education.

It is a fact, of course, that on an individual basis it is more difficult for some individuals to teach in one area or level than in another. For example, an individual with lack of aptitude, skill, and talent in the science area would most likely not become a college science teacher but might well become, let us say, a high-school English teacher. Now for anyone to generalize that college science teachers are brighter than high-school English teachers would seem to be unrealistic. Likewise it would appear unjustified to suggest that college science teachers are making more significant contributions to education simply because they teach at a higher level.

But let us look at what appears to be a more obvious difference between teaching levels: the high-school teacher versus the elementary-school teacher. There are those who strongly believe that high-school teachers are brighter, have more difficult challenges as teachers, and require more in-depth preparation. Although these people very seldom verbalize it, they also feel that in general secondary teachers are superior to elementary teachers.

I am not suggesting that these are necessarily the feelings of secondary teachers. On the contrary, the myth is circulated by several groups of people. Some elementary teachers disseminate the myth themselves when they comment, as I have heard them, "I am only an elementary teacher." In other groups, the myth may sound something like this statement directed at an elementary teacher by a parent, "How much longer would you have to go to school if you wanted to become a high-school teacher?" Some administrators and school boards make their contributions to the myth through decisions that are made about salary, work load, and a host of other such areas; these decisions clearly suggest that one group has a more difficult and challenging set of tasks than the other. Do you agree?

In examining this myth in greater depth and justifying its placement in this chapter as a myth, I would like to have you examine the following standards and goals for teachers.

A teacher is an individual who makes effective use of his or her "self" by interacting with: others, available media, materials, organization and management schemes to facilitate learning—the development of potential development of a behavior by students.

A "good" teacher is a teacher who facilitates student learning effectively and efficiently, and in such a manner that the learner expresses and exhibits a desire to continue development and engagement with the learning opportunities available to him.

A "poor" teacher is an individual who is ineffective and/or inefficient in facilitating learning, and/or facilitates learning in such a manner that the learner expresses and/or exhibits a desire not to continue development and engagement with the learning opportunities available to him.

The aims, goals, objectives of the———teacher education program are to plan for, facilitate, and evaluate the development, without coercion, of individual students into autonomously motivated, functioning teacher candidates who:

1. Know elements of, and relationships within, the socioeducational matrix—such as the historical, current, and projected content and values of the matrix.

2. Know their "selves" with respect to the social matrix, which means their perceptions, knowledges, values, energies, abilities, attitudes, goals, techniques, developmental progress, and probable future growth.

3. Know the structure or organizing themes of the academic disciplines and possess a working knowledge of academic content usually found in the———school program.

4. Know educational organization and management schemes.

5. Know a variety of alternative educational methods, techniques, mediums, materials, and resources suitable for facilitating learning.

6. Know the characteristics and norms that facilitate learning in children and adults. These characteristics and norms are primary as they relate to the effective functioning of school programs.

7. Are well-informed individuals above and beyond being an———teacher.

8. Are capable active-reactive social participants, that is, not passive and not offensive in most situations.

9. Are able to suggest, analyze, synthesize, evaluate, develop, and implement learning alternatives relevant to a given situation and to themselves as educators.

10. Are able to make decisions and choices among alternatives consistent with a given "self" or set of "selves" and known educational objectives.

11. Are able to continue their educational and professional development beyond the formal college program.

Does it become readily apparent to you, as you read these general overall goals, what type of teacher we are talking about? Could these goals apply to a college math teacher, a junior-high social-studies teacher, or an elementary teacher—filling in the blanks with certain terms that relate to each area and level? For this author, the answer is yes.

Education is a continuous process from birth to death and is the responsibility of a number of people. To say that one level of teaching is more important than another for those who are professional educators is indeed a fruitless exercise. This author would rather suggest that there are a variety of different vantage points from which to make a contribution as a professional educator. Different vantage points require different levels of preparation and skill, aptitude, and ability; to suggest that one level is more important than another is untrue. As Raymond Harris points out in his stimulating analysis, *American Education: Facts, Fancies and Folklore:*

> Although it is natural for any teacher to consider his own assignment as the most complex of all, the art of teaching is substantially the same at all grade levels. Because whatever is taught must be taught to human beings, the same professional skills and understandings are essential everywhere, and the need for teachers with culture and intelligence is universal.[3]

The Carbon Copy Teacher

Still another myth about classroom teachers and teaching, although not as immediately noticeable, is the belief that all teachers in any given subject area are basically the same in terms of teaching style and general overall behavior. English teachers are all alike, math teachers are generally cut from the same mold, elementary teachers are similar and so on down the line. Again we are faced with, in this author's opinion, an outdated and unrealistic perspective on the teacher. Teachers like the students they teach vary greatly both in personality and teaching style and, in today's teaching world, it is more difficult if not impossible to generalize about the personal qualities and teaching style of teachers at various groups and levels.

Consider, for example, Bob Nelson, Mary Gibson and Leonard Shark, three junior-high-school social-studies teachers from three different communities.

First of all, there is Bob who is 24 years old and a teaching

3. Raymond P. Harris, *American Education: Facts, Fancies, and Folklore* (New York: Random House, 1962), p. 102.

veteran of three years. Married and a father of two children, Bob enjoys working with junior-high-school students and is very active in all dimensions of school life. He works with the track team, assists with the school dramatics program, and is a faculty sponsor to many student activities and organizations. In addition to school responsibilities, Bob spends much time with his family and friends enjoying the outdoors. Among his favorite hobbies are hunting, fishing, golfing—in fact, almost any type of team or individual sport you can name. In the classroom Bob appears to be most at home professionally. Even an observer can see the tremendous amount of physical and mental energy that Bob puts into his teaching. A firm advocate of inquiry-oriented instruction, Bob teaches so that his classes are usually dominated by a high percentage of student involvement of a variety of sorts.

Just last Tuesday, for example, Bob initiated a unit of study on the Soviet Union in one of his eighth-grade classes in the following manner: "Jack, come on up here to the front and help me get this class started today. I need your help, and besides you always wanted to be a teacher anyway, didn't you?" (Class laughs as Jack finds his way to the front of the room and Jack is smiling right along with his classmates and teacher. They all seem to feel comfortable in the situation. To an outside observer it is obvious that such activity is not new to Bob Nelson's classroom.) "Jack, how about you and I putting on a little two-man production for the rest of the group that I hope will be helpful in getting us to think about our next area of concern?"

(Bob takes two chairs and puts them side by side in the front of the room, then he and his student, Jack Katz, sit down. Bob holds a copy of a large city newspaper.) "OK Jack, I would like you to imagine that you and I are complete strangers riding side by side on the subway." (Class laughter is again heard.) "All right, now these subways are noisy enough so the rest of you will have to hold it down so you can hear."

(After brief laughter the class appears ready for "the production," and Bob Nelson, burying himself in the newspaper, leads off the conversation.) "Boy oh boy, the more I read about things going on in this world of ours the more depressed I become. Things are really bad all over aren't they?" (Poking Jack with his elbow.)

"I guess so." Jack replies not really feeling a part of the production at this point.

"I mean, just look at all the news about wars and conflicts all over the world. I think it's those Russians, don't you?"

Jack, still not quite with his role, goes with the "I guess so" reply.

"What do you mean, you guess so: they are really bad, aren't they? Like what have they ever done for us? Nothing except trouble I tell you. The whole lot of them." A careful observer might note at this time that Bob Nelson is studying carefully the nonverbal reaction of his class. Some of the students indicate agreement with the position offered, others seem confused, and some obviously want to state, "Hold on a minute."

This seems to be Jack's frame of mind as he now begins to swing with the production by saying, "Well, I don't really think you can say they are all bad. . ."

This teaching episode leads to an active class discussion around such questions as: What do we really know about the Soviet Union? Why would we want to study about it? What type of things would be most important to study about? etc.

Mary Gibson, also a junior-high-school social-studies teacher, like Bob can be considered active in many dimensions of school life. Mary, 34, is married and has three children. She is very active outside the classroom as well and enjoys skiing, bowling, reading, and camping activities with her family. In the classroom, however, even an amateur observer could point out striking differences between Mary's and Bob's classroom style. She takes on a very businesslike approach to her classroom teaching and you can almost predict in advance what will be going on in her classroom before you enter. She also just recently initiated a unit of study of the Soviet Union and it went something like this: "All right, class, as I told you yesterday, today we are going to begin a study of the Soviet Union. As you all know, it is very important that we know a great deal about this country as it effects us in many ways and is likely to continue to do so in the future. I asked you to read the first six pages of the unit in your text. It gives you some of the major reasons why the study of the Soviet Union is so vital in today's world. I thought we might start today by discussing some of these reasons. Susan, what do you. . ." And so the episode goes.

Our third social studies teacher, Leonard Shark, teaches his classes and that's about the extent of his involvement in school activity unless he is required to engage in other school activities. Married and the father of one child, Leonard spends most of his spare time reading and involving himself wherever possible in local politics. He is a frequent contributor to Letters to the Editor and regards himself as a liberal in the midst of a group of conservatives.

25

Mr. Shark also talks about the importance of student involvement and feels that more school time should be devoted to student discussion and activity. His approach to the study of the Soviet Union was first to provide his students with background material on the country by lecturing for the first three days. Following the lecture, the class was then divided down into groups to discuss the material presented. This cycle would be repeated with new topics and as a matter of fact in almost any unit that Leonard Shark was teaching.

So there you have three junior-high-school social-studies teachers; although no one will pretend that the sketchy information provided about them is adequate for really identifying their teaching style, it is obvious that they indeed are different and unique. As Harris points out, "Teachers are different, of course. But they are infinitely more different from one another individually than from the general public as a whole. . . . Like people in general, teachers come in all sizes, shapes and ages, pursue all manner of interests and avocations, and exhibit the widest range of personality types and behavior."[4]

Some believers in the myth that all social-studies teachers are alike add another dimension—that it is in fact desirable for teachers to behave in certain similar ways in order to be successful. To lecture is bad, to have discussion is good. To stimulate questions is good, to simply answer them is bad. To have colorful bulletin boards is good, to have bare walls is bad. To use a multimedia approach is good, to use single media is bad. To smile is good, to frown is bad. To work in small groups is good, to teach to a large

4. Ibid., p. 83.

group is bad. To use supplementary materials is good, to use a single text is bad, etc. Actually this list could be extended in many ways for there are many conceptions of the methods, techniques, and specific behaviors that a "good" teacher should reflect. Without a specific teaching context, however, it would be unwise to try to pass judgment on, say, the use of classroom exposition by a teacher rather than inquiry-oriented group discussions. For some instructional goals, classroom exposition or lecture, if you will, is completely justified and appropriate; for other goals, completely inappropriate. Therefore, for a teacher to attempt to adopt one technique at the expense of the other only limits the teacher's range of strategies—and they need so many to deal with the complex range of teaching situations and problems on a day-to-day basis.

Teaching is extremely personal in nature; this author feels it is a myth to believe that there is one type of desirable carbon-copy style that must be part of a teacher's makeup within a given subject or level. You might use your own background as a case in point. Who are the good teachers you have had the good fortune to work with? Were they alike? "If one thinks back to his own school days, one will probably remember that the good teachers one has had in one's life did not all behave alike or even with great similarity. Rather, each stands out as a person, an individual, some for one reason, some for another. Each had his own peculiar methods, values, and techniques. Good teaching is like that, an intensely personal thing."[5]

The Uninvolved Teacher

A final myth in need of comment is the belief that teachers are basically self-contained members of their communities and, for the most part, non-community-involved individuals. Although it is still difficult for teachers to take part in certain community functions, such as organizations that meet during the school day, there is no question but what the teacher is becoming a more active element in all aspects of community life.

Teachers have been elected to various positions in local government, including the position of mayor in some communities. Teachers are active also in state and national political activities. Teachers are actively involved in local and district churchwork and hold responsible positions on governing boards and committees. Conservation activities in various areas usually have teachers serving in some capacity. Civic music, YMCA, recreation activities, League of Women Voters, local bowling teams, civic planning commissions and advisory groups, fine art groups and community theater are all places and organizations where you will find teachers involved and at work.

Indeed, teachers are active in most communities and expect to be considered full-fledged members of the community in every way; this will vary from community to community, of course. For people to generalize that

5. Arthur W. Combs, *The Professional Education of Teachers* (Boston: Allyn and Bacon, 1965), p. 7.

teachers only teach and socialize among themselves is clearly another aspect of an outdated perspective.

Other myths about teachers and classroom teaching that could be mentioned include the teacher as a task master, the teacher as "neutral" on controversial issues, the teacher as the sole classroom decision maker, the teacher as a conservative, and right on down the line. Whatever the myths may be as you or I see them, one thing is certain—a changing society and a changing educational environment will no longer tolerate the image of teacher radiated through such myths. Clearly a new concept of teacher is called for, one which embraces the best of what we have conceived a teacher to be in the past together with the new elements of image and role demanded in the future. These will be the focal points of concerns in future chapters, but first let's hear from the learner.

QUESTIONS FOR ANALYSIS

1. What myths, in addition to those mentioned in this chapter, do you feel exist about classroom teachers? Do you question some as being myths? Do you regard some myths as more serious than others? Explain your answers.

2. What impact has the knowledge explosion had on the world of teaching?

3. Should all teachers be willing to share "cracks in their own humanity" as they work with learners at all levels? What about the person who is unable to do so? Should he be a teacher?

4. What do you think could be done to break down the myth that teachers who work with older learners are "superior" teachers because "they need to know more"? Do you feel that some individuals choose a certain teaching level because of this myth?

5. Is it possible for someone who has had a serious problem with drugs or alcohol to become a teacher? Why or why not?

6. Describe two very different types of teachers you have had, both of whom you regard to be excellent teachers even though they are completely different in style.

7. Should teachers remain neutral on controversial issues in the classroom? Why or why not?

8. What are some of the unique qualities you feel you will bring or have brought to the teaching profession? What are some uniquenesses you have observed in others?

9. In the future, what major changes do you anticipate regarding the teacher's role?

SELECTED REFERENCES

Anderson, Robert H. *Teaching in a World of Change.* New York: Harcourt Brace Jovanovich, 1966.

Chandler, B. J., Powell, Daniel, and Hazard, William R. *Education and the New Teacher.* New York: Dodd, Mead, 1971.

Combs, Arthur W. *The Professional Education of Teachers.* Boston: Allyn and Bacon, 1965.

Harris, Raymond P. *American Education: Facts, Fancies, and Folklore.* New York: Random House, 1961.

Henderson, George, and Bibens, Robert F. *Teachers Should Care: Social Perspectives of Teaching.* New York: Harper & Row, Publishers, 1970.

Kohl, Herbert R. *The Open Classroom: A Practical Guide to a New Way of Teaching.* New York: Vintage Books, 1969.

La Mancusa, Katherine C. *We Do Not Throw Rocks at the Teacher!* Scranton, Pennsylvania: International Textbook, 1966.

Ohles, John F. *Principles and Practice of Teaching.* New York: Random House, 1970.

Silberman, Charles E. *Crisis in the Classroom.* New York: Random House, 1970.

Skeel, Dorothy J., and Hagen, Owen A. *The Process of Curriculum Change.* Pacific Palisades, Calif.: Goodyear Publishing Company, 1971.

28

NOTES

29

THE
TEACHER:
The Learner's Perspective

A teacher is person Who Will Teach
US, how too Read and Rite. he Will
Sometimes talk With US Whan
We ned help. Sometime a teacher
Will get mad at us. A teacher is
JuST a person So he can make
mistakes. Just like you and me.

"A teacher is just a person so he [or she] can make mistakes," too. This sincere and provocative thought is shared with us by an eight-year-old girl as she responds to the question: What is a teacher?

This is not a new thought of course, but the style of the young lady, misspellings and all, together with her direct and honest approach to the task at hand, reminds us of the importance of the learner's perspective on this question as well as on others relating to education. For this reason it was decided to offer at this point the learner's concept of teacher. I hope you will rediscover, as I have, the refreshing sharpness—of various dimensions of the teacher's role—that only the language of children and young adult learners can provide.

The learners' comments found on the following pages represent various levels of education from nursery school through post-doctoral fellows. They are representative of learners in many types of learning environments ranging from inner city to rich suburban school settings; from large schools to small schools; and from traditional classrooms to progressive open concept classrooms. Some of the comments are cute and clever, some searching, some are light and happy in style and others weighted with seriousness. Some are painfully direct. *All are honest and sincere* and contain messages of various sorts for teachers, but you be the judge.

Teacher Versatility

For example, what does Tommy's statement say to you as he offers his nine-year-old perspective on the concept of teacher?

1. "A teacher is a man/woman that is nice sometimes and teaches five year olds up to gronups. A teacher teaches math, science, biology, maps, and all sorts of things.

2. "Sometimes they are nice and sometimes not. A man/lady that does almost anything."

Do teachers "do almost anything"? Should they? Should one of the qualities of a teacher be versatility? Do students basically hold teachers too high on a pedestal, particularly at the early stages of schooling? For example, does Linda, a third-grade student, give too much credit to the school as the only source of learning?

"A teacher is someone who helps you learn. And if there wher no teachers there would not be any schools and with out schools we would not know any thing."

Or how about Kari's statement?

"A teacher is someone who work's more then a student does. Because they have to plan the math problems and what they are going to do in sicince and maps. If teacther's wernt here I gess we wedent know anything because they teacth us all we know. Teacther's are mitey helpfull you know."

Is it natural for children to feel that the teacher is the source of all learning? Would you want the children in your class to feel that way about you? What do teachers do that contributes to such attitudes by young learners? Would you try to change such a concept of teacher if one of your students felt that way about your role as a teacher? How would you go about it?

The Teacher as Helper

The helping concept of teacher is also in the perceptual field of many young learners. Note the following responses which illustrate a variety of ways in which children feel teachers are helpful:

"A teacher is a friend. A teacher is a person who helps children learn. Go to a teacher and he or she will help you. Thats what a teacher is."

"A teacher is someone that has to like kids at least a little. A teacher helps: you wouldn't believe it. A teacher spends almost as much time with you as your parents during the school year. A teacher has to know quite a bit and has to go to college for a few years. A teacher can be a man or a woman. It doesn't matter. There are a lot of college students trying to become teachers. Some come to watch and learn things from kids in school. They learn a lot. Many teachers have helped me, boys and girls. Teachers have good days and bad days; usually good, but some are bad. Teachers have it pretty rough when they don't feel good or just can't keep the class quiet. I feel sorry for them when things like that happen. I like recess, but when we come in it's hot and miserable for us and the teachers. I like teachers. They go through a lot, but that's what they wanted to be so I respect them. I think I might be a teacher. . . and then again I might not."

"A teacher is someone that helps someone learn to understand things better in school and out. Students in school are sort of teachers in a little way because they are helping their teachers to understand them better. I think anybody that teaches somebody something is a sort of a teacher. They also help with mistakes you make."

Even the child in nursery school views the teacher as a helper. As four-year-old John expressed it:

"A teacher helps you. . .you know, she helps pass out the snacks."

My Teacher

It is interesting to note that when the teacher is viewed as a helper, the concept of teacher shifts from a focus on a person to a focus on a function. Students can help people learn too, and as one youngster so aptly expressed it, "any one who helps you learn something is sort of a teacher." There are professional critics of education who feel quite strongly about this point and who urge a movement away from formal school settings which have teachers and learners. They would prefer to see learning left to society in general, allowing various segments, individuals, institutions, etc., to contribute in natural ways to the education of the people. Compulsory education is one of the immediate prime targets of such critics. What are the basic issues that surround such a point of view? Where do you stand as a teacher or a prospective teacher? But more on such issues later so as not to stray from our immediate purpose: the child's frame of reference.

"Nice" Classroom Teachers

Being nice is another qualification or characteristic that the young learner regards as important in his concept of teacher as might be noted in the following comments offered by elementary students.

"A teacher is not a person who puts us in a row. He [she] is not the one and only teacher. In my *opinion* a teacher is a person who likes kids; a teacher is a nice person. In my school a teacher is a nice person who will help you when you have a problem, not a math problem but a friend problem. Maybe your friend does not think you like her so she makes friends with other people and leaves you out. But a teacher says it's good to make other friends, but it's bad to leave you out. So you talk and he makes you feel better. I like boy teachers and girl teachers. They are both nice. Some teachers approach subjects different ways. They tell how the other guy feels. The End."

"I think a teacher is to help us learn things we will be using in the future.
"They are nice. They help us when we have trouble with our work.
"They talk to us and don't get mad. They are understanding and if we have homework, they expect them on time but don't bug us if we don't hand them in on time.
"I think teachers are good just the way they are."

"A teacher is nice sometimes. When they let you go to the store. If they let you smoke. Some are mean and think they are our gaurds."

"A teacher should have a smile on his or her face almost at all times. A teacher is a person who shouldn't swear, bring relitives to school or talk about them and favor any one student or make fool of them."

"A teacher should be funny and nice. What I like in a teacher is what she teaches us. What I want in a teacher is happiness and joy."

"A teacher is a person that teaches you something. A teacher is a person that helps you with your problems. A teacher helps you do things. A teacher is a nice person. A teacher brings new thoughts into your mind. A teacher is a nice, sympathetic person. Sometimes he trys to help you but he really can't. Sometimes he will confuse you, but he helps alot. He's a good thinker. Sometimes he makes you mad. He's glad to help you."

"A teacher is a person who should come to school with a smile and not angry because of some problems at home. A teacher should have patience with his or her students so they can learn more easily. A teacher shouldn't favor any student if they can help it."

"A teacher should *always* answer when called upon unless they are busy. "Teachers shouldn't talk about their personel likes unless it pretains to the subject.
"A teacher shouldn't swear in front of his students."

36

"Some teachers are mean and some teachers are nice and the kind of teacher i like is nice."

How does your concept of being nice relate to the ideas offered by these children? How will you bring happiness and joy to your students and how important do you think it is to do so? Can you have a smile on your face

all of the time? Should you? How will you handle days when you do bring "problems from home" into the classroom? Where is your patience level? What do you think about the child's comment that "teachers help you learn things you will need in the future"? Children give us a lot to think about, don't they?

"A Very Smart Person"

Teachers are also viewed by young children as "very smart" and, by the sound of some of their comments, nearly invincible.

"A teacher is a helpful person. I think a teacher is a person who is very thoughtful and very kind. A teacher does all the work planning things for the students who screw everything up for the teachers. Teachers are the smartest person in the room. A teacher get's mad sometimes and I see why. A teacher is good to a student. A teacher is understanding. A teacher is nice. And the teacher is brave, strong. Teacher's are kind-hearted."

"I think a teacher is souposed to be a very smart person. They shouldn't make very many mistakes (really none at all). Yet teachers do make mistakes and children laugh and that may embarrass the teacher. Even though they do I still like my teacher."

T H E
N
D

"Mean and Bossy" Teachers

All children of course don't view the teacher as someone who is helpful, nice, and the "smartest person in the room." On the contrary, teachers are viewed by some children as downright mean, bossy and, in the words of one young fourth-grade lad, "smart alecs." But let the children tell you themselves:

"A teacher is a person who bosses you around. Makes you do what they want you to do. Its pretty sickening when they say I had to do it when I was in school, and I had to go to college to be a teacher. They think they're so big because they can boss you around, kick you out of class etc."

"A teacher is a person who always gets mad when people do what they shouldn't do. Like talking, shouting, running. Cause when they talk to much you know what happens you say 'good bye gym' or 'good bye lunch' and if you still talk you start getting hungry and hungrier. And sometimes its a week of gym which don't make the students any happier.

But if you come back from reading or math or social studies or anything and sit down and be quiet, you won't miss a whole week of gym or get hungrier and hungrier by going to lunch late."

"A teacher is a person who gets so goll darn mad. And if you get a pencil from your neighbor you get yelled at for just getting a pencil. At least you can go to the bathroom without getting yelled at. If you could at least go outside about three times a week. And if we could sit by anybody we wanted but we would have to be quiet."

"Teachers are helpful and nice sometimes. And when the teacher says something the students have to obey. Teachers are the worst emny of students. Teachers get mad fast and they swear to. And when you asked him something sometimes he does it. And if the teacher gets mad our gym will be taking away for the day or week. And we always pick up the floor every night. When he's in a good mod we don't do much work. If he is mad we have to do work, work and work all day."

"A teacher is someone who bitches at you to do some work. They teach you about many different things. Most of it you never heard before. A teacher is a person who talks to you about anything you want to know and some of them you can tell your problems to. Teachers are not that bad. There only mean to you if your mean to them first. Then they are really nice."

For those of you who might have in some way been concerned or shocked by the concept of teacher shared above, I highly recommend skipping over the following examples which are even more direct, more critically penetrating, more "colorfully" illustrated but no less sincerely offered by upper-elementary and junior-high-school learners.

XXXX XXXX Teachers!

"A teacher is a person who likes a lotta of money. Dosent really care bout the students she is teaching. There not very responsible. They think they are always rite. Can't face up to their own problems they take it out on the kids. They are Predujuce about induvals. In other words they are a BITCH."

"A teacher is someone that helps you learn.
  helps you get in trouble
  brakes up good fights
  but. . . . some of them can be nice but most of them are a bunch of big mouths, they show off around other people, they act as if they own the whole world. There so sick I can't see how any one can stand them
    but they can be ok

    SOMETIMES."

"A teacher isnt vary respensble, a teacher theimks they no everything they always take their problems out on the kids.
theachers are prgidest

IN OTHER WORDS THEIR ALL
    PRICKS"

"I think a teacher is:

1. Some are nice.

2. Most are mean.

3. Most they think they are hot shit.

4. They act like we are in prision for murder, and they are our gaurd's.

5. Some are reall nice and dont get mad all the time.

The intensity of one young lad's response can only be shared by examining his own manuscript, which has been torn and punctured a hundred times with his pen point, as he shares his concept of teacher.

What is a teacher

It is some son of a bitch that makes you work.

How do you, or how will you, respond to learners with such feelings about teachers? What are the contributing factors that lead to such perceptions of teachers and what they do? Are you prepared to deal with such attitudes? How will you approach such problems?

Student-Teacher Relations

The teacher's relationship with students is another area of concern reflected in the young learner's concept of teacher. For example:

"I think teachers should sit down and talk things over with their students and they should try and reason with the kids."

"A teacher should be patient and also should try to be there when a student needs them mostly. They should explain the assignment so every student understands it. Understand each student and help those who are a little slow.

"When a student does something wrong the teacher should sit down and find out why the student did it. Not just bring them out in the hall with a stick. There is no way in which the student or the teach could ever understand each other.

"Sure the student might stop doing it but why? The student isn't sure and the teacher is never sure that the student has learned anything. He might just turn around and next year do the same thing.

"Teachers should also have controll over there class at all times. This is true in some cases."

"A teacher talks to kids. They yell at me sometimes and sometimes it's not fair. A teacher gives me ideas. He is like water on a desert sometimes when I need him. A teacher is nice when he is in a good mood. A teacher is like a senator in the world politics."

"A teacher is someone to correct you in mistakes.

"A teacher is someone to learn from, to copy.

"A teacher is mean when you don't cooperate.

"A teacher is nice when he or she is in a good mood.

"They don't like you talking in class.   41

"They want you to look at them.

"They feel you are learning sometimes when you're not.

"They feel that when your with your friend, you don't work. I don't think so.

"Sometimes I don't think it is fair all the time to yell at students.

"I don't like it when teachers force things on you, even when they suggest things. They act like you have to do it.

"Sometimes they act like they're in the primary for best teacher."

"A teacher is a person who supposedly teaches children.

"Sometimes teachers forget what it was like to be a student."

Teachers do forget sometimes what it is like to be a student. This of course is all the more reason why we need to solicit student reactions and perceptions. These reactions should not be limited to the young learner but should include learners at all levels. For example, what do the following concepts of teacher say to you as they are offered by high-school, college, graduate and post-doctoral learners?

The Adult Learner Responds

An undergraduate teacher-education major states:

"A good teacher must first recognize that each person is a unique individual who should be helped to develop a definite idea of who he is, and his unique place in society in relation to his heritage and his future.

"A good teacher should never lose sight of the fact that the people she will have the privilege to influence have many needs. I believe five of these must be recognized. First, and most obvious of course is his *physical* welfare, which to some degree will determine his emotional stability. Second, she must learn to deal with the *emotions* of her students. (It is hoped by this time she has learned to deal with her own.) Third, with so much emphasis on the personal pursuit of learning there could be a danger of short changing the *social* aspect of it. Interaction with his peers on a scholarly as well as purely recreational level is mandatory. Fourth, a healthy child will enjoy a *mental* challenge and probably feel uneasy if everything were so easy. The fifth dimension is the *spiritual.* I realize that whatever belief, or none, the child has, most likely came from home. This is good and the teacher should never discuss ideologies with the intent to influence her students in a public school. But there are basic values she can teach such as politeness, kindness, sharing and consideration for her and the other students. (Her example is probably the best teacher in this case.) Helping her students understand people is just as important as the content she teaches."

42
A high-school senior relates:

"Qualities a teacher should have are honesty, devotion, loyalty, patience, love. What the teacher does with these makes the teacher.

"When a teacher can inform students on material the students want that's great. The teacher should be a guide. A teacher should not monopolize any class. If the teacher is honest, respect and understanding, which is essential, will develop. If a teacher is devoted to her position and task, classrooms will be exciting and fun. If the teacher is loyal, considering what children need now and not what they'll need next year—loyalty means she won't sneak up and deceive them. They will get what they need. What is a teacher without the patience and love with children? It is not possible to have too much love and patience."

A teacher in the field states:

"First of all, a teacher must be human. A willing listener, an alert observer, and a responsible guide.

"One who promotes a classroom atmosphere of open-endedness; who permits individuals to remain individuals at the same time promoting cooperation and responsibility."

Patience becomes an important dimension of a parent's concept of teacher:

"A teacher is a person who is dedicated to the needs of others. A teacher must put the needs of her (his) students first. She should be equipped with a large reservoir of patience and understanding. She often has to be parent, counsellor, and friend to the student. Probably the most important thing a teacher must learn is to understand and be able to relate to the student—whether the student be 5 years or 50 years."

What do the following undergraduate and graduate student statements say to you as a teacher or prospective teacher?

"A teacher is a person who guides the learning of a child. He is there to help along but not to force his ideas on a pupil. The teacher should be a person to whom a pupil can easily turn to when the need arises. He should be able to make the child understand that when decisions have to be made the child must make them under guidance of the teacher.

"A teacher must be kind and understanding. A child should be able to feel he can approach the teacher at any time with any problem and not be subjected to sarcasm."

"He or she should have a sense of humor. One who knows how to laugh at appropriate times. Facial expressions are important. Love for the student should be written on his or her face. It is important that a student knows that his teacher cares for him as an individual. A teacher should be happy, because if a teacher is happy, the students will be happy.

"A teacher should have knowledge in all areas or know how to obtain knowledge. A teacher should admit if he or she does not know something. Honesty is a good policy.

"A teacher should have an over abundance of enthusiasm and interest in whatever he or she is doing.

"A teacher should be a guide in all learning situations."

"A teacher is a professional person who helps other people, mainly younger people, to learn. A teacher should be one who is patient and understanding and is willing to give of his time and energy whenever the need arises whether it be during school hours or otherwise. He should be a person who likes to work with young people. A good sense of humor is always an asset to a good teacher. He should be a guide and leader rather than a dictator. In fact, a teacher has to play many roles during his teaching career."

Several of the "older" learners, who have experienced a larger number of teachers in their background, commented on the multirole aspect of teachers:

"A teacher is a counselor, a mother, a nurse, a bundle of uncapped energy that can be dispensed at the slightest command of a youngster. She is above all a listener, sensitive to the climate of each of her individual charges and must be able to communicate by thought, word and deed."

"My concept of a teacher is a 'resource guide.' He is resourceful to the extend he has a certain amount of knowledge to share with the student.

He is a guide to the extent that he can show students where to find 'knowledge,' whether to be intangible human relationships through relations with students, or more tangible things like facts which may be found in books, films, lectures, etc."

"A teacher plays a temporary, facilitating role in the learning process. He should know when to tap in on students' own individual spontaneous ways of learning, how and when to help, and when to step aside. A teacher should be as excited about learning as he expects his students to be. He should be willing to be unappreciated or forgotten in the excitment accompanying the learning he sets into motion."

"When I was in grade school a teacher was mainly a disciplinarian. They never had time for anyone and was always very stern. The teachers were never regarded as a human being but rather someone to be incensed up on a pedestal. You did what they wanted when they wanted you to do it. One slip and that was the end of you. For some years now that idea has changed. First of all, the teacher is a human being. The teacher is not just in the classroom to babysit and discipline but is rather someone who is there to be your friend; someone who is willing to give you her best and guide you to be a person not only intellectually but socially and emotionally. You are treated as an individual and the teacher is there—interested in you, ready to help."

"A teachers main task is to guide youngsters in the learning process. They should have, or strive to have, a repore with the students that allows unrestricted communication.

"I believe that teachers still must set an example in conduct, manners, etc. The 'Do as I say and not what I do' thing is one of the worst attitudes a teacher can have.

"One last thing—a teacher must be conscious of his relationship to the community. I feel he can be one of the better salesman for good education and school-community relationship."

So there you have a representative sampling of the learner's concept of teacher. I am sure you will agree that there is a high level of correlation between the thoughts of learners and the professional educators' views on what the role of teacher is or should be. There may even be a new dimension or two added by the children and young adults. Several of these statements, I am sure, were offered for our benefit as teachers and perhaps do not reflect the true perceptions of the learner. But then, even a "reported perception" is more valuable than no perception at all and it is in this spirit that the comments of learners have been offered.

You will need to devise your own techniques and methods for soliciting the perceptions of your own students. Despite your best efforts however, many things will remain a mystery. As one fifth-grade student stated:

"A teacher stands for a lot of things—but I don't feel like writing them."

QUESTIONS FOR ANALYSIS

1. Do you feel it is important to seek out the learner's perspective on issues related to your role as teacher? If so, how will you tune in to their ideas? How will you solicit them? What will you do with them?

2. Some individuals talk of the importance of maintaining a professional distance from students so you will be more objective in helping them with their work in school. You must not, they say, become too friendly with the students. How do you feel about this matter? Is it possible to be too friendly with students?

3. Should learners make more responsible decisions about what they do in school than they appear to be making at the present time? If so, what type of decisions should they make? How could you help facilitate greater decision-making options for your students?

4. What would you anticipate to be the most difficult aspect of having more direct and constant feedback on your teaching by your students?

5. What type of comments would you like your students to make most frequently about your instruction? What type of behavior on your part would most likely contribute to a student's motivation to offer such statements?

6. How often have you voluntarily offered feedback to teachers you have worked with, pro or con? What factors contributed to your making these written or oral statements or to withholding them?

SELECTED REFERENCES

Actually the most significant references I can suggest for you in this area are your own students' written statements about your teaching and about education in general. They are ready to write, *if you are willing to ask them.*

NOTES

THE
TEACHER:
A Picture is Worth a Thousand Words

If by this time you do not have as complete a picture of the changing role of the teacher as was intended in the first three chapters, perhaps a visual time line would be appropriate for reinforcing important points. Then we will take the next steps forward in examining in greater detail specific dimensions of the concept of teacher.

QUESTIONS FOR ANALYSIS

1. What basic thoughts came to your mind as you reviewed the pictorial time line of teachers and teaching? What changes were evident? What additional changes could be illustrated with other photos or drawings?

2. If you were to continue this time line into the future, what type of photos do you think would or could be included?

SELECTED REFERENCES

Johnson, James A., compiler. *History of Education in Color Slides.* DeKalb, Illinois: Creative Educational Materials. 500 slides.

59

NOTES

THE
TEACHER:
New Demands in a Changing Role

The winds of educational change blow strong today in America.
For more than a decade, great cumulonimbus clouds of educational
reform have been blowing back and forth across the United States.
To what extent have these clouds nourished with their fresh
moisture the fields below?[1]

1. John I. Goodlad, M. Frances Klein, and associates, *Behind the Classroom Door* (Worthington, Ohio: Charles A. Jones, 1970), p. 3.

The statement cited above from a 1970 analysis of schools and classrooms might well have been offered a century ago, because the cry for educational change and reform has been constant throughout educational history. It would in fact be possible to trace and identify the "cumulonimbus clouds of educational reform" as early as the golden age of Greece, from the 470s to about 300 B.C., and for that matter even prior to that period of time. To do so, however, would be an exercise in macrology and, as viewed by this author, distracting from the major focus of this book. Such detailed perspectives of historical educational reform movements can be noted in the stimulating works of L. A. Cremin, H. G. Good, and D. B. Tyack.[2] Collectively they trace the educational rumblings, or the "clouds of reform," created by such individuals as Comenius, Francis Bacon, John Locke, Rousseau, Horace Mann, John Dewey and his disciples William H. Kilpatrick and John Childs. The "rumblings" of such educational reformers, and many others not mentioned, was uniformly loud and vigorous as they protested against pedagogical narrowness and inequity in the educative process. Unfortunately the response to their cries for reform was also, in this author's opinion, uniformly slow, unresponsive, and for the most part ineffective in bringing about the type of changes that were being pleaded. To be sure, schools and education were improving with each passing year but not nearly at a pace or with the quality that most educators would have deemed desirable.

61

The 70s—Same Challenge, a New Response

The cloud formations of the 70s are not all that different—educational reform continues to be called for by articulate spokesmen and critics such as Charles Silberman, John Holt, Paul Goodman, Herbert Kohl, Jonathan Kozol, Carl Rogers and others.[3] Their cries for reform as they castigate American schools, although couched in contemporary terms, are not unlike those of their predecessors. But there appears to be a new and refreshing response to the cry for reform. Unlike earlier periods of time when the response to pleas for reform were greeted by a smattering of experimental

2. Lawrence A. Cremin, *The Transformation of the School* (New York: Alfred A. Knopf, 1961). H. G. Good, *A History of American Education* (New York: Macmillan, 1962). David B. Tyack, ed., *Turning Points in American Educational History* (Waltham, Mass.: Blaisdell, 1967).

3. Paul Goodman, *Compulsory Mis-Education* (New York: Vintage, A Division of Random House, 1969). John Holt, *How Children Fail* (New York: Pitman, 1967). J. Holt, *How Children Learn* (New York: Pitman, 1969). J. Holt, *The Underachieving School* (New York: Pitman, 1969). J. Holt, *What Do I Do Monday?* (Dutton, 1970). Herbert Kohl, *The Open Classroom* (New York: New York Book Review, Dist. by Vintage Books, 1969). Jonathan Kozol, *Death at an Early Age* (Boston: Houghton Mifflin, 1967). Neil Postman and C. Weingartner, *Teaching as a Subversive Activity* (Delacorte, 1969). Carl Rogers, *Freedom to Learn* (Merrill, 1969). Charles Silberman, *Crises in the Classroom* (New York: Random House, 1967).

programs spread thinly throughout the educational arena, today's response appears more intense, more vibrant, and more widespread. Indeed the same dynamic quality which has characterized change in the British schools and transformed nearly two-thirds of Britain's infant and junior schools into more personalized open classrooms, seems to be gripping American education. Although the pace is more deliberate (as perhaps it should be) it is nevertheless more consuming than ever before and the extent to which the "clouds of educational reform are nourishing the fields below" is indeed encouraging.

This activism can be noted in a number of ways. For example, many schools are breaking with time-honored traditions in their quest for more personalized, humanized, and individualized programs. This change is occurring not only in the rich, the large, and the experimental schools but also in the small schools. Nor are these reforms to be found only on the east or west coasts, which in the past have been regarded by many as the seedbed areas of educational change. On the contrary, rural North Dakota villages are the scene and source of exciting educational change. As a matter of fact the changes that appear to be taking place in the "out of the way" school districts are perhaps the most significant in the current educational reform movement.

Other apparent responses to the cry for reform can be noted in the new directions taken by professional publishers; they are developing instructional materials which are more varied and personalized in style and content. Then there are the new positions assumed by various professional organizations which appear to be driving hard and firm in their attempts to influence change. Lay groups and organizations are becoming more aggressive, spurred on by themes like "accountability" and also by the economic crunch which is forcing a reordering of priorities in schools. Performance contracting is a reality in many school districts. Changes in teacher education programs aimed at "practicing what you preach" are also part of the total scene which is alive with activity.

But perhaps the most encouraging aspect of all is the changing attitudes of teachers and students. Today, more than ever before, we are seeing students and teachers, individually and collectively, questioning the relevancy of many aspects of what goes on in and around schools. They are asking the "why" questions and offering the "why not" alternatives as they examine their roles and the roles of others in the educative process. Such aggressive, spirited, and sincere revolutionary responses are indeed welcome on the educational scene. This mood of willingness to acknowledge weaknesses and to consider new alternatives might well be the readiness stage for major changes if we can successfully translate our ideas into action.

An Attack on Joyless Schools

It is not difficult to find common focal points from among the major criticisms leveled at American education. In general the critics appear to be saying:

Schools are too conservative;

Schools are teacher dominated;

Schools in the main are dull, lifeless places where activity is too far removed from the real world of the learner;

Schools encourage conformity rather than creativity;

Schools fail to capitalize on the social subsystem which they represent;

Schools operate with large amounts of instructional materials which have never been systematically tested and evaluated prior to use;

Schools place too much emphasis on the values of learning for adult years rather than the here and now in the lives of students;

Schools do not provide the learner with enough opportunities to make responsible decisions about things that affect his life;

Schools are geared too much toward the what, when, and where and not enough toward the why and how;

Schools are not flexible enough;

Schools do not encourage diversity but in fact deny it through many school policies and procedures;

Schools are in too many instances *joyless.*

Silberman refers to the joyless quality of schools and states that:

It is not possible to spend any prolonged period visiting public school classrooms without being appalled by the mutilation visible everywhere—

mutilation of spontaneity, of joy in learning, of pleasure in creating, of sense of self.

He goes on to point out that:

because adults take the schools so much for granted, they fail to appreciate what grim, joyless places American schools are.[4]

Children themselves provide the same type of information if given the opportunity. As one sixth-grade student put it when asked for his reaction about school:

"I wouldn't go to school if I didn't have to. The teachers are always telling you what to do and we can never do anything that's fun. All you do is sit and listen to them talk, and talk and talk. We always have to raise our hands for everything, walk in straight lines, go to the bathroom at the same time. We have to learn so many things and I don't know what for.

"Many times I will think to myself is this subject I am studying really worth it? Will it be any use to me when I grow up? Well I don't really know because I have not grown up yet. But I sure hope the teachers know what they are doing.

"The teachers don't like my ideas and they think I am dumb. cause I am not as good as the other kids. I will show them when I quit.

"I don't like school."

Although the words may tumble over one another in one place or another, the message is crystal clear.

Another perspective on the need for a reordering of the schools' relationship to the real lives of children can be noted in Stephen Corey's "Poor Scholar's Soliloquy." Although this soliloquy of a seventh grader's view of school is, in part, a humorous commentary on school practice, there can be no doubt that its underlying message is for the most part painfully accurate.

No, I'm not very good in school. This is my second year in the 7th grade and I'm bigger and taller than the other kids. They like me all right, though, even if I don't say much in the schoolroom, because outside I can tell them how to do a lot of things. They tag me around and that sort of makes up for what goes on in school.

I don't know why the teachers don't like me. They never have very much. Seems like they don't think you know anything unless they can name the book it comes out of. I've got a lot of books in my own room at home—books like Popular Science Mechanical Encyclopedia and the Sears' and

4. Charles Silberman, *Crisis in the Classroom*, p. 10.

Ward's catalogues, but I don't very often just sit down and read them through like they make us do in school. I use my books when I want to find something out, like whenever Mom buys anything secondhand I look it up in Sears' and Ward's first and tell her if she's getting stung or not. I can use the index in a hurry to find the things I want.

In school, though, we've got to learn whatever is in the book and I just can't memorize the stuff. Last year I stayed after school every night for two weeks trying to learn the names of the Presidents. Of course I knew some of them like Washington and Jefferson and Lincoln, but there must have been thirty altogether and I never did get them straight.

I'm not too sorry though because the kids who learned the Presidents had to turn right around and learn all the Vice Presidents. I am taking the 7th grade over but our teacher this year isn't so interested in the names of the Presidents. She has us trying to learn the names of all the great American inventors.

I guess I just can't remember names in history. Anyway this year I've been trying to learn about trucks because my uncle owns three and he says I can drive one when I'm sixteen. I already know the horsepower and number of forward and backward speeds of 26 American trucks, some of them Diesels, and I can spot each make a long way off. It's funny how that Diesel works. I started to tell my teacher about it last Wednesday in science class when the pump we were using to make a vacuum in a bell jar got hot, but she said she didn't see what a Diesel engine had to do with our experiment on air pressure so I just kept still. The kids seemed interested though. I took four of them around to my uncle's garage after school and we saw the mechanic, Gus, tearing a big truck Diesel down. Boy, does he know his stuff!

I'm not very good in geography either. They call it economic geography this year. We've been studying the imports and exports of Chile all week but I couldn't tell you what they are. Maybe the reason is I had to miss school yesterday because my uncle took me and his big trailer truck down state about 200 miles and we brought almost ten ton of stock to the Chicago market.

He had told me where we were going and I had to figure out the highways to take and also the mileage. He didn't do anything but drive and turn where I told him to. Was that fun! I sat with a map in my lap and told him to turn south or southeast or some other direction. We made several stops and drove over 500 miles round trip. I'm figuring now what his oil cost and also the wear and tear on the truck—he calls it depreciation—so we'll know how much we made.

I even write out all the bills and send letters to the farmers about what their pigs and beef cattle brought at the stockyards. I only made three mistakes in 17 letters last time, my aunt said—all commas. She's been through highschool and reads them over. I wish I could write school themes that way. The last one I had to write was on, "What a Daffodil Thinks of Spring", and I just couldn't get going.

I don't do very well in school in arithmetic either. Seems I just can't keep my mind on the problems. We had one the other day like this:

> If a 57 foot telephone pole falls across a cement highway so that 17 3/6 feet extend from one side and 14 9/17 feet from the other, how wide is the highway?

That seemed to me like an awfully silly way to get the width of a high-way. I didn't even try to answer it because it didn't say whether the pole had fallen straight across or not.

Even in shop I don't get very good grades. All of us kids made broom holders and a bookend this term and mine were sloppy. I just couldn't get interested. Mom doesn't use a broom anymore with her new vacuum cleaner and all our books are in a bookcase with glass doors in the parlor. Anyway, I wanted to make an end gate for my uncle's trailer but the shop teacher said that meant using metal and wood both and I'd have to learn how to work with wood first. I didn't see why but I kept still and made a tie rack at school and the tail gate after school at my uncle's garage. He said I saved him $10.00.

Civics is hard for me, too. I've been staying after school trying to learn the "Articles of Confederation" for almost a week because the teacher said we couldn't be good citizens unless we did. I really tried, because I want to be a good citizen. I did hate to stay after school, though, because a bunch of us boys from the south end of town have been cleaning up the old lot across from Taylor's Machine Shop to make a playground out of it for the little kids from the Methodist home. I made the jungle gym from old pipe and the guys made me Grand Mogul to keep the playground going. We raised enough money collecting scrap this month to build a wire fence clear around the lot.

Dad says I can quit school when I'm fifteen and I'm sort of anxious to because there are a lot of things I want to learn how to do and as my uncle says, I'm not getting any younger.[5]

Do you feel the message is appropriate in the 70s?

There can be little or no doubt that the attack on joyless schools in the 70s and beyond will be vigorous and will be waged by teachers, students, administrators, and the lay public alike; the extent to which we can

5. Stephen M. Corey, "The Poor Scholar's Soliloquy," *Journal of Childhood Education* 20 (1944): 219.

confront the basic issues as a team will, I am sure, contribute to the overall degree of success we can hope for. Commitment and conviction are essential.

Joyless schools will not be eliminated by a change in textbooks, a new course of study, a juggling of the time schedule, by implementing a new organizational model, or by any one of a hundred additional individual items that could be added to this list. It will require a major reordering of priorities and total commitment and conviction of those involved with the education of children. As Carl Rogers states:

> When we put together in one scheme such elements as a prescribed curriculum, similar assignments for all students, lecturing as almost the only mode of instruction, standard tests by which all students are externally evaluated, and instructor-chosen grades as the measure of learning, then we can almost guarantee that meaningful learning will be at an absolute minimum.[6]

Most promising is the present attack on schooling that is narrow, restrictive, and remote from the real needs of the learner, but the battle has just begun. All we can predict with any degree of certainty at this point is that the central issue of the 70s will be the

> struggle to assert truly human values and to achieve their ascendancy in a mass, technological society. It will be the struggle to place man in a healthy relationship with his natural environment; to place him in command of, rather than subservient to, the wondrous technology he is creating; and to give him the breadth and depth of understanding which can result in the formation of a world culture, embracing and nurturing within its transcending characteristics the diverse cultures of today's world.[7]

This is no small task but the signs are encouraging.

6. Carl Rogers, *Freedom To Learn* (Columbus, Ohio: Charles E. Merrill, 1969), p. 5.

7. John I. Goodlad, "The Future of Learning: Into the 21st Century," *AACTE Bulletin* 24, no. 1 (March 1971): 4.

The Open Classroom, an Alternative

One exciting and encouraging response to the plea for educational reform has been the writing and experimentation surrounding the open classroom concept of schooling. Although there are many different definitions of open schools and classrooms, there does appear to be a common bond of characteristics which provide a general frame of reference. Generally speaking, open schools and classrooms are characterized by:

A wide range of learning opportunities for children with multidirectional goals.

The absence of prepared curriculums, competitive marking systems, and uniform materials for all children.

A concept of education which is broader than the school: education as life, not education for life.

Children stimulating each other to productive learning experiences—not only teacher stimulus.

The absence of straight rows of desks with the teacher in the front of the room—rather an apparent physical environment exists with children engaged in activities of a variety of sorts in a variety of different areas.

An emphasis on children knowing themselves.

Instructional activities that are based on real problems and interests of children.

A warm and genuine sense of respect for children and their life space.

Greater responsibility placed on the student's shoulders for his work in the school environment.

An emphasis on the here and now focus of learning and a reduction in emphasis on learn now—use later.

An emphasis on learning rather than teaching with variable times for learning rather than fixed times.

The absence of compartmentalized learning in favor of natural integration of subject matter within the framework of real life problems of children.

An emphasis on process over product in the learning of the child.

Happy children who enjoy going to school.

The impressive list of characteristics cited above, I am sure, will be viewed as Utopian by some readers, and viewed by others as not significantly different from earlier conceptions of what the school should be. Both views are to be respected, but neither are to be accepted as good reasons for lack of progress toward such goals. It would appear that educators have all too frequently taken one of these two positions at the expense of trying to get closer to this concept of schooling in actual practice. But things are changing and the handful of such schools that exist in the United States and, on a much larger scale, in Great Britain are promising.

Leonard Sealy, a pioneer in the British Open School movement, commented recently in a lay journal about the transition in education that has come about recently in Great Britain. He related that:

> In Britain the most important thing is that we've given the schools to the children. There are too many influences bombarding children today which they can't escape—violence and persuasion on TV right in their living rooms, the pressures of competition throughout the society—and they've no retreats in which they can just be children. There are no closets to hide in in a small apartment and grandmothers usually live too far away. The schools had to become a haven in which children could be *children*. Not long ago, all our schools were rigid, sterile environments in no way suited to children and it was no wonder kids getting out of them wanted to biff somebody on the nose. We have found that children can and do make choices on their own with a great degree of skill and wisdom and that if allowed to do this they will learn deeply and well. In England, it seems the battle may have been won; in America, only the early skirmishes are being fought.[8]

69

The teacher, as always, remains one of the key elements in the American educational movement toward openness. It will require larger numbers of gifted teachers to "win the battle" as James Koerner points out:

> We've found out that informal methods alone do not produce results comparable to those we get in using determined and structured programs to educate children in the basics of human knowledge. This "classical" approach assumes that adults know better than children what they are going to need to know and that they simply coerce them into being literate and competent to make decisions. What I call the "romantic" approach—which basically is what is being used in Britain—is all well and good in the hands of a gifted teacher. But ours is a mass system: you can't transplant the British methods unless you have sufficient teachers of comparable ability.[9]

8. Leonard Sealy, "Classrooms Alive With Chaos," *Life*, April 1969, p. 56. Barbara Villet, LIFE Magazine, © 1969 Time Inc.

9. James Koerner, "Classrooms Alive With Chaos," *Life*, April 1969, p. 56. Barbara Villet, LIFE Magazine, © 1969 Time Inc.

Phillip Tennison, a creative teacher in an experimental open school,[10] builds on many of the characteristics cited above as he offers his concept of an open classroom:

> Open schools might, in fact, open opportunities for both the learner and the teacher to see themselves in different roles. The learner might see that the responsibilities, the decisions and the consequences are increasingly his. The teacher might see that he is, increasingly, the facilitator and decreasingly the determiner in the learning process.

> The process of education must be between the learner and what is to be learned. We must also remember that the interaction between the learner and what is to be learned is constantly occurring. A teacher today must be a person who aids in this process of education. My teaching responsibility then is to keenly observe this interaction and this learner and to help in making decisions about the elements that enhance this process. These include learning styles, appropriate content, predictive sequencing, environment, grouping patterns, etc. In performing these important tasks I hope to put an emphasis on guiding, assisting, helping, listening, and encouraging. I hope to minimize actions labeled determining, demanding, disseminating, directing and leading. Natural authority prevails when I truly have something pertinent to offer the learner at the appropriate time.

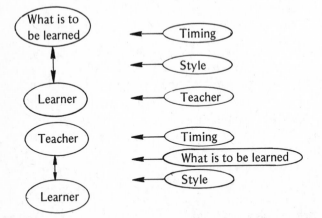

Obviously trying to carry out this concept has some very rewarding moments and some very frustrating hours. The best days however come from having a stimulating environment in which children are offered several alternatives if they need several and the openness to build their own alternative plan if they are able. A stimulating environment must also

10. Phillip Tennison, Intermediate Unit Leader, Thomas Gray Campus Laboratory School, St. Cloud State College, St. Cloud, Minnesota.

imply that the child feels secure, challenged, and worthwhile as a productive member of that group.

How does your definition of an open classroom compare with this classroom teacher's concept? Is it the style of classroom you want as a teacher? What are the prospects for the future? Is the open classroom a realistic dream?

Silberman, despite his findings about the joyless qualities of most American schools, has hope and is optimistic. He finds the experimentation with the open classroom encouraging and in a speech at the 1970 Annual Convention of the National Education Association, as reported in the *AACTE Bulletin*, he concluded that the schools can:

be humane and still educate well,

be genuinely concerned with gaiety and joy and individual growth and fulfillment without sacrificing concern for intellectual discipline and development,

be simultaneously child-centered and subject- or knowledge-centered,

and stress aesthetic and moral education without weakening the three R's.[11]

What kind of teachers will be needed to allow such classrooms to develop and flourish?

New Demands on the Teacher's Role

To assume that the open classroom is the only model available to replace typical current school practice would indeed be foolhardy. By the same token it would be absurd to suggest that a new model of a teacher is needed to replace an old model. Such a position would grossly underrate the creative master teachers of the past and the current teachers who indeed reflect in practice the soundest of teaching strategies and leadership as they work with students at all levels. But it would likewise be foolhardy to fail to point out the growing number of challenging new demands on the role of a teacher for the 70s and beyond. It is a changing world of teaching and for anyone considering education as a career it is imperative to look at the hard, cold facts on current demands and challenges for such a role. These demands and challenges are numerous and stem from several sources.

There is, for example, the demand that teachers in the future be held more accountable for their work with children and youth. Lay groups and the profession itself are suggesting and following through with implementation of progress reports, sharper and more precise evaluation systems, and a

11. Charles Silberman, "Charles Silberman on Alternatives to Crisis," *AACTE Bulletin* 24, no. 1 (March 1971): 8.

host of other techniques which clearly make the classroom teacher more visible and responsible to the community and school. Questions like What progress has my son made in the last six weeks and what has contributed to this or detracted from it? How can you justify the use of such materials in your classroom? How can you prove to me that a sex education program is part of the school's responsibility and not that of the church and home? Why aren't you spending more time on reading instruction in your classroom? are only a representative sampling of the type of inquiries being directed at teachers. The question, What did you do at school today? is indeed no longer reserved for the student.

Another challenge for teachers in or entering the field today is the team approach. Team teaching, nongraded organizational structures, and even the open classroom call for, and are dependent on, new adult relationships in which teachers work, plan, and interact with other teachers and adults in their work in the school. The day of the hidden classroom teacher in her own room with thirty children is clearly fading and in its place a complex network of human interactions is being formed with all of the rewards and frustrations that accompany two or more human beings working closely together. There are the satisfactions of sharing with others yourself as a person, your ideas, the joys that surround teaching, and much more. On the other side of the coin there are the frustrations of personality conflicts, backbiting, power struggles, and a host of other problem areas. Many adults will be able to accept this. Some will find it threatening. All who choose teaching will have to live and work with such concerns as it is clearly a real world dimension of the profession. Are you willing to face this challenge in the 70s?

The teacher of the future will also have to be a resourceful person, for along with the accountability movement will come a tightened instructional budget within which to operate. Local taxpayers' associations are providing leadership for a reappraisal of the relationship between dollar input into education and values derived, and for the teacher this once again means justify and account for. A reordering of priorities will clearly be a part of the teacher's job as he or she seeks new resources and modified use of existing resources in working with children.

The world of pressure will also be larger and more pronounced for the classroom teacher in the 70s. As we have already noted, community and lay group pressures will continue to mount as the public dissects the school and its teachers. Students themselves will create new pressures as they too question the relevancy of their experiences in school and demand a stronger voice in the educational decision-making arena. Then there will be the teacher—teacher pressures brought about by teaming, by competition in merit pay systems, and numerous other ways. Teacher-administrator relations are also being strained as new hierarchies are being created in schools and as the teachers are demanding stronger voices in school decision making. These are only a sampling of the day-to-day sort of pressures that the teacher will need to confront in his work. The ivory tower world in which the teacher is in full control of a relaxed, secure environment for herself is clearly a myth; to expect such a world would be unrealistic.

And there is so much more. For example:

Teachers will need to be more skillful in helping children learn how to learn, for the role of teacher as the storehouse of knowledge to be shared has long since passed us by because of the knowledge explosion.

The teacher will need to be broad in background, for the fine lines which have separated math, science, social studies, and other areas will be dissolved in schools of the future and the role of teacher will be to assist in bringing significant content and processes to bear on real problems. It will not come in packages.

The teacher of the future will have to be more open as an individual, willing and uninhibited about sharing both her strengths and weaknesses as a real person and not as a stereotyped image called *teacher*. She will have to learn to be herself and not to pretend to be something to fill out a role.

The teacher of the 70s will need to feel comfortable in learning as well as in teaching, for her role will at times place her in the learner's position. She will pursue goals with her students and many times learn from the children in the process. She will not know all the answers in advance.

The teacher of the future will also have to be a good listener, for the pattern of dialogue in the school environment will shift to the students. We will be taking more instructional leads from students and, to do so, we will need to hear more from them. Teachers will need to take seriously the expressions of children and learners at all levels.

The teacher of the 70s will need to become more active and more passive simultaneously. More active in terms of stimulating, guiding, and mediating, and more passive in terms of doing everything for his students. Students should assume more responsibility for their own learning and be the most active agents in their own education. To allow this to happen we will need teachers who are willing and eager to release some of the time-honored power that has normally been associated with the role of teacher.

Being able to face controversy and live within it is a quality also called for in teachers of the future. The role of teachers and education in a new social order for the 70s and beyond is, and will continue to be, filled with controversy and the teacher will be called upon on numerous occasions to defend and justify educational positions of all sorts. How will you behave in such situations?

A professional teacher of the future will also need to possess qualities which will assist her in making more instructional decisions than ever before from a much larger cadre of options.

To be able to deal effectively with a professional environment that is in the midst of rapid and major change will also place demands and challenges before the teacher of the future. Movements away from prescribed curriculums to programs built around the expressed needs and interests of the learner; changes in the physical environments within which teachers work; new discoveries about the way children learn; and rapid developments in the use of technology in teaching are only samples of the changing educational world that teachers will live in in the 70s. How will you or how do you fit into such a dynamic profession?

To sacrifice, openly and genuinely as a human being, will be a demand relating to the changing role of the classroom teacher. If we are to deal with the major issues of our times in our schools—like race relations, crime, drugs, and the problems of a rapidly deteriorating physical environment— we will need to deal with them as activists. Teachers will need to do more than talk about such issues and assume passive "outside viewing" roles, they will need to illustrate through their own behavior that they care and that they follow through with their caring by doing all they can about them. Are you willing to get involved? Are you willing to make sacrifices —real ones, major ones, not token efforts?

Schools without walls, lighted schools, and the community school movement will also create new demands for teachers. One basic demand will be for teachers to be community educators as well as educators of the student population. Schools will be open nights, weekends, and during the summers, and the community will on numerous occasions look to the teachers for leadership and help in some areas. Are you willing to respond? Can you look beyond the contracted services to respond to the needs of adults in your community as well?

Although it may sound more like a boy scout motto or slogan, the teacher of the future will need to be brave in many ways, or to put it more bluntly, will need to have guts. To respond to a need a given student might have by offering a genuine hug or embrace, which communicates the affection needed, will not be easy for a teacher knowledgeable about the teacher in the next community who is being sued for child molesting because he or she touched children. Likewise it will not be easy for teachers to allow and encourage students to discuss controversial issues in class when she knows pressure groups are watching her every move. Can you handle it?

These challenges and demands, which are a part of the real world dimensions of the teacher's role for the 70s, are only the start to a list which is most complicated and awesome. Perhaps no one would fit such a set of shoes, but to fail to try them on for size would be a real mistake. Some dimensions of this role will be more natural to you than others. Some you will need to work hard to develop and nurture. Others are perhaps beyond your grasp. As a professional educator you will always be reaching and stretching out toward such goals, which will constantly be changing.

In the next section of this analysis some of these dimensions of the teacher of the future will be isolated and examined in greater detail to assist you in finding your own handle to these most pressing concerns.

QUESTIONS FOR ANALYSIS

1. What do you consider to be some of the major reasons why change has come so slowly to many aspects of education, when the cry for change has been constant throughout educational history?

2. Who do you consider to be some of the major change agents of our times? Why do you feel they are?

3. What are some of the other new options in addition to the open school concept? How can some of the teachers who are operating in other school models join in the attack on joyless schools? *How will you join in the attack?*

4. What do you consider to have been the most significant development in American education in your professional lifetime? What are the reasons for your choice?

5. What criticisms do you feel are being leveled at American education in addition to those outlined in this chapter?

6. What should be the teacher's role as a change agent in the school and in the more general arenas of American education?

7. What are some of the major problems that will be related to the open school movement?

8. In what ways have you experienced pressure as a teacher or as a student? How did you respond to this pressure?

9. What new demands do you see being placed on teachers in the 70s and beyond?

SELECTED REFERENCES

Anderson, Robert H. *Teaching in a World of Change.* New York: Harcourt Brace Jovanovich, 1966.

The British Infant School. Dayton, Ohio: Institute for Development of Educational Activities, 1969.

Chandler, B. J., Powell, Daniel, and Hazard, William R. *Education and the New Teacher.* New York: Dodd, Mead, 1971.

Chilcott, John H., Greenberg, Norman C., and Wilson, Herbert B. *Readings in the Socio-Cultural Foundations of Education.* Belmont, California: Wadsworth, 1968.

Corey, Stephen M. "The Poor Scholar's Soliloquy." *Journal of Childhood Education* 20 (1944): 219.

Cremin, Lawrence A. *The Transformation of the School.* New York: Knopf, 1961.

Cullum, Albert. *Push Back the Desks.* New York: Citation Press, 1967.

Dennison, George. *The Lives of Children.* New York: Random House, 1969.

Frost, Joe L., and Rowland, G. Thomas. *Curricula for the Seventies: Early Childhood through Early Adolescence.* Boston: Houghton Mifflin, 1969.

Glasser, William, M.D. *Schools Without Failure.* New York: Harper and Row, 1969.

Good, H. G. *A History of American Education.* New York: Macmillan, 1962.

Goodlad, John I. "The Future of Learning: Into the 21st Century." *AACTE Bulletin* 24, no. 1. March, 1971.

Goodlad, John I., and Klien, M. Frances. *Behind the Classroom Door.* Worthington, Ohio: Charles A. Jones, 1970.

Goodman, Paul. *Compulsory Mis-Education.* New York: Vintage Books, 1969.

———. *New Reformation: Notes of a Neolithic Conservative.* New York: Vintage Books, 1970.

Herdon, James. *How to Survive in Your Native Land.* New York: Simon and Schuster, 1971.

Holt, John. *How Children Fail.* New York: Pitman, 1964.

———. *How Children Learn.* New York: Pitman, 1969.

———. *The Underachieving School.* New York: Pitman, 1969.

———. *What Do I Do Monday?* New York: Dutton, 1970.

76

Koerner, James. "Classrooms Alive With Chaos." *Life* April 1969.

Kohl, Herbert R. *The Open Classroom: A Practical Guide to a New Way of Teaching.* New York: Vintage Books, 1969.

Kozol, Jonathan. *Death at an Early Age.* Boston: Houghton Mifflin, 1967.

Lessinger, Leon. *Every Kid a Winner.* Palo Alto, California: Science Research Associates College Division, 1970.

Neill, A. A. *Summerhill.* New York: Hart, 1960.

O'Neill, William F. *Selected Educational Heresies.* Glenview, Illinois: Scott, Foresman, 1969.

The Open Plan School. Far Hills Branch, Dayton, Ohio: Institute for Development of Educational Activities, Inc.

Postman, Neil, and Weingartner, Charles. *Teaching as a Subversive Activity.* Delacorte Press, 1969.

Rathbone, Charles, ed. *Open Education: The Informal Classroom.* New York: Citation Press, 1969.

Rogers, Carl R. *Freedom to Learn.* Columbus, Ohio: Charles E. Merrill, 1969.

Rogers, Vincent R. *Teaching in the British Primary School.* New York: Macmillan, 1970.

Ryan, Kevin, and Cooper, James M. *Kaleidoscope: Readings in Education.* Boston: Houghton Mifflin, 1972.

——— and ———. *Those Who Can, Teach.* Boston: Houghton Mifflin, 1972.

Sarason, Seymour B. *The Culture of the School and the Problem of Change.* Boston: Allyn and Bacon, 1971.

Sealy, Leonard. "Classrooms Alive With Chaos." *Life* April 1969.

Silberman, Charles. "Charles Silberman on Alternatives to Crisis." *AACTE Bulletin* 24, no. 1. March 1971.

———. *Crisis in the Classroom.* New York: Random House, 1970.

Skeel, Dorothy J., and Hagen, Owen A. *The Process of Curriculum Change.* Pacific Palisades, California: Goodyear, 1971.

Toffler, Alvin. *Future Shock.* New York: Bantam Books, 1970.

Tyack, David B., ed. *Turning Points in American Educational History.* Waltham, Mass.: Blaisdell, 1967.

78

SECTION TWO

Multiple Dimensions of Classroom Teaching

As we have noted, there are many dimensions to a teacher's role. The purpose of Section Two is to examine several of these roles in greater detail to provide an opportunity for teachers and prospective teachers to frankly confront the real world of classroom teaching and to examine their role in that world.

Chapter 6 probes the quality of genuineness as related to the professional role of a teacher. The importance of teachers being themselves as opposed to "trying" to act like teachers will be the central theme and through a series of classroom episodes the reader will be introduced to many of the problems and issues that relate to this teacher quality.

The teacher as mediator is the focus of Chapter 7 where a major experimental project involving primary children is discussed. The project relates to a child decision-making model in which the role of teacher as mediator is highlighted.

Can teachers really motivate students to learn? This central question is explored in Chapter 8, which focuses on motivation and the role of the teacher. Chapter 9 explores the scholarly dimension of the teacher's role.

The final chapter in Section Two attempts to sort out crucial issues in the decision-making role of today's classroom teacher. The types of decisions which are demanded, a few modest guidelines for decision making, and a set of episodes where you can practice your decision-making competency are among the areas explored.

80

THE
TEACHER:
On Being Genuine

The educational function does not rest upon our ability to control, or our will to instruct, but upon our human nature and the nature of experience.[1]

1. George Dennison, *The Lives of Children* (New York: Random House, 1969), p. 246.

Carl Rogers in his stimulating analysis *Freedom To Learn* states that "when the facilitator [teacher] is a real person, being what he is, entering into a relationship with the learner without presenting a front or a facade, he is much more likely to be effective."[2] This of course is not a new idea, for concerns about the importance of teacher genuineness are as old as educational activity—and as time-honored. Research over the years has also, without serious question, supported the idea that a measure of one's success as a teacher is related to his genuineness in working with the learner. But what does it really mean to be genuine as a classroom teacher? How would you point out the quality of genuineness, or lack of it, for those teachers you have been associated with in the past?

To me, genuineness starts with self-concept and the teacher's willingness to expose herself as she really is; her feelings, attitudes, beliefs, and personal and professional values as they might be appropriately related to educational activity. It is being herself and no one else. It is being real. It is being comfortable with personal strengths and weaknesses and not being threatened by them. It is being free from needing to create impressions of being more than you really are.

To illustrate, consider the example of Mary Olson, a first-grade teacher meeting her class for the first time. Twenty-five sets of eyes look her over; there are some smiles, some frowns; some children look out the window, some are already restless from being seated for two minutes, some chat with one another. What about Mary? She looks a bit tense, or should we be more honest and say that she looks scared to death?

Let's watch her for a moment as she takes that first big step forward. "Well now, this is a fine-looking group if I ever saw one. Are you happy to be back in school again?" (Mixed reactions ranging from loud no, no,

2. Carl Rogers, *Freedom to Learn* (Charles E. Merrill, 1969), p. 106.

no and yes, yes to just a slight eye movement from those children who are obviously a bit uneasy on this the first day of school.) "You know, it's kind of hard for me to really tell how you feel about being back in school, can you tell how I feel?" This question brings a quick reply from one of the boys who really hasn't noticed Miss Olson's nonverbal reaction of being afraid, which has not gone unnoticed by many other children. "You are happy to be back. All teachers like school."

Miss Olson replies: "Well, to tell you the truth I am happy to be here but I am a little bit scared too. You know, this is my very first class and when I came to school today I thought to myself: I sure hope my class likes me." Already visibly more relaxed, Mary continues by saying, "I suppose some of you came to school today wondering what school would be like too and what I would be like as your teacher. It's funny how that works isn't it? . . ." and on into the first day of school goes Mary Olson, not quite as afraid as before and perhaps with a few children who had also shed some of their fears because Mary was willing to expose her feelings openly.

Contrast this with another teacher, Janet Hall, who we will place in exactly the same situation. Janet's approach is quite different from Mary's in that much of her concentration is aimed at the goal of disguising her obvious feelings of fear from the children: "OK class, if everyone will find a seat we will get started." (Long pause as children get settled and Janet circles the group with a white-knuckled grip on her record book and a posture which makes every inch of her five-foot-five frame illustrate *I am the teacher.*) "OK, let's see if we can get to know one another. The first day of school is always so exciting for me and it's so much fun to find out what everybody has done during the summer months. Let's start in this row by going around and finding out what everybody did this summer." If Janet had taken time to really look at the children, she certainly would not have missed the fact that the boy who was to lead off the sharing was in about the same state of affairs that she was—scared stiff. But on the sharing went, until she came to Susan who just shrugged her shoulders in embarrassment. At this point, when some of the other children began to laugh, Janet's tension became the controlling factor in her behavior and she began lecturing the children on the importance of respect for the feelings of other people. Even to an untrained observer it became obvious that Janet was doing all she could to hide her own feelings and in the process was creating uneasy feelings within the children in her group through her exaggeration of the situation. She was trying very hard to "act like a teacher" and in the process was becoming less and less like her real self. Janet also wanted her class to like and respect her but after her first few hours with the group she knew her progress toward that goal was at a complete standstill.

It is indeed unfortunate that many professionals in the field feel they have to "act like teachers" in some way in order to fulfill that role. We see it in the teacher who comments on the importance of maintaining professional distance from the students so as not to lose their respect. This is the kind of teacher who will resist a spontaneous hug or embrace, which is a natural response to some educational activity or experience in or related to the classroom. This teacher finds it hard to share experiences like the excitement of a local-team or individual victory, the tragedy of the death of an individual close to a student, an embarrassing moment for either the student or the teacher, the joy and excitement of completing an educational experiment that has met with positive results, the relief that comes when a student, who is depressed or troubled with a problem, talks about it freely. It is strange indeed that such physical contact as a pat on the back, an embrace, or sitting a six-year-old on your lap are viewed by some teachers as acts which are not appropriate for teachers.

It would seem that a teacher who did not take advantage of her full range of communication vehicles, including physical communication, to interact with students is robbing many of the children she or he works with. For one youngster it is enough *to tell* him how proud you are of him for an accomplishment, for another the thought may never be communicated without the accompanying arm around the shoulder and broad smile. For one child it may be enough *to say* you are interested in listening to him read and talk about his story; for another, his being seated on your lap is a prerequisite for really knowing he has your undivided attention and interest. In the negative context, simply to comment on your feeling of disappointment to one student may be adequate; for another, the physical contact of placing your hands on the student's arms as you share this feeling is the key to communication.

For others "to act like teachers" means never to expose your weaknesses to children and to the best of your ability to be a bright shining star in your classroom at all times. Frankly I know of no one who is capable of attaining such a goal (even if it were worthy of attaining which obviously can be seriously questioned). Everyone has weaknesses, many of which are difficult to disguise, and the only continually shining stars are those among our heavenly bodies. What children need in teachers are real people who with their strengths, and despite their weaknesses, can help children and youth grow and develop. This does not mean acting like somebody; it means being somebody who is genuine. As Kohl points out:

> In an open classroom the teacher must be as much himself as the pupils are themselves. This means that if the teacher is angry he ought to express his anger, and if he is annoyed at someone's behavior he ought to express that, too. In an authoritarian classroom annoying behavior is legislated out of existence. In a "permissive" classroom the teacher pretends it isn't annoying. He also permits students to behave only in certain ways, thereby retaining the authority over their behavior he pretends to be giving up. In an open situation the teacher tries to express what he feels and to deal with each situation as a communal problem.[3]

3. Reprinted with permission from *The Open Classroom*, A New York Review Book, 1969. Copyright © 1969 Herbert Kohl.

To deal with each situation as a communal problem is a challenging task and it may even be unrealistic to hold our expectations that high. All teachers cannot behave in this manner; we know that all teachers are not alike, for we have already commented on the uniquenesses of teachers. On the other hand it is clear that, as teachers, we seem to miss opportunities to deal openly with problems and issues which relate to what we really are as individuals as opposed to what we are when we play out a role. Several questions might be raised which illustrate the point. For example:

Should teachers share openly any fears they have with their students such as fear of certain animals, fear of the unknown, fear of height or high places, fear of failure, or whatever. What values might be derived from such sharing of oneself? Under what circumstances would such sharing be most profitable, least profitable?

Should teachers speak freely with their students about how they feel on any given day—tired, happy, irritable, sad, or whatever the feeling? Should teachers ever share feelings of anger and disappointment about students with the students directly?

Do you feel that teachers should ever indicate to students that they like some areas of teaching more than others? Should they ever relate aspects of their work that they just don't like at all?

Should teachers ever talk about their own basic weaknesses as individuals or the major and minor mistakes they have made in the past like cheating, stealing, undesirable behavior toward others, etc.? What conditions would justify or not justify such behavior on the part of classroom teachers?

Is it ever justifiable for a teacher to shout at children or to strike them in any way?

Is it ever defensible for a teacher to hug or kiss a student or vice versa? Again, what circumstances would justify or not justify such behavior? Is there enough physical contact both from a positive and negative standpoint in our classrooms?

Should teachers ever express their personal positions on controversial issues like the war, birth control, politics, etc.? Why or why not? In what way?

Although all of the questions are obviously out of context in one way or another, it would be this author's position that in most instances a "yes" answer would be quite appropriate. Of course, it is realized that the wide range of uniquenesses among teachers would make it difficult, if not impossible, for some to behave in this fashion. But for many it is possible and, in this author's opinion, highly desirable. Let us use a classroom illustration.

Bob Larson is a sixth-grade teacher in a suburban school district. If you had been in his classroom three weeks ago, you would have heard the following exchange between Bob and some of his 28 students as they were discussing the topic of honesty.

Judy: Have you ever been dishonest, Mr. Larson?

Mr. Larson: Yes, I have. I suppose everyone has been dishonest at one time or another in their life. I remember one time when I was about your age I was sent to the store to purchase some groceries for my mother. I asked her if I could have a dime to buy something at the store. She said not today. So I went to the store and I bought some candy anyway and then I made up a story about how I lost some of the money on the way home.

Larry: Boy, I bet your mom got mad at you, eh?

Mr. Larson: Well not really. She asked me if I was sure that I really lost it and I said yes. Then she said she believed me and I really think that her trust in me after I had been dishonest with her was much worse than her getting mad at me. I can remember how uneasy I felt and later the same day I had to tell her and we had a long talk about it.

Larry: I bet you were never dishonest again?

Mr. Larson: I wish I could say that, Larry, but I really can't. Even though I think I know better, I have sometimes been dishonest as an adult too. About three years ago, for example, I bought a new suit and when the salesman undercharged $10.00 I didn't say anything about it even though I knew he was not charging me enough. I didn't get around to going back and correcting my account until two weeks later and I thought about it a lot during those two weeks. Now why do you suppose I would have done a thing like that when I really knew better and that was being dishonest? Why do you think people in general, children and adults, sometimes do things that are dishonest? Have you ever done anything dishonest? Why? How did you feel about it?

(And on went the discussion)

There are some individuals who would say that Bob Larson should never have shared such information about himself in a classroom situation because he would automatically lose the respect of his students and because he might be teaching children to be dishonest in the process. Such is not the case, at least in this author's opinion. On the contrary it would seem that Bob Larson has provided the children with the rare opportunity to learn to respect him for what he is as an individual, strengths and weaknesses as well. It may be that the personal strength of being willing and comfortable about sharing your weaknesses in some way helps compensate for the weakness itself. This of course is not to justify the weakness but to put it honestly in perspective. And what should respect for an individual be based on? What he really is or what he pretends to be?

As for teaching the children to be dishonest, there is some question that a teacher's honesty can teach dishonesty. It would seem that at the heart of the issue of honesty is the personal confrontation with the reasons for dishonest behavior (unless you really believe that there are individuals who have never in any way been dishonest) and your response as an individual to such temptations. In the illustration cited above, Mr. Larson's behavior may have cleared the way for some children in his room to begin to deal openly with their world of temptations and the mistakes they may have made in that world. You are asking a great deal of children if you expect them to open up if you are unwilling as a teacher to do so.

Kohl points out that the teacher as a human being "has as much right to be angry, frustrated, impatient, distrustful as the students have and should let them know that." He feels

> if you are angry with a student for fighting or for refusing to do what you **87** want him to do, tell him and try to deal with the question of why you are angry. If someone tears up a book of yours express your feelings about it to the student. Only when a teacher emerges as another person in the classroom can a free environment based upon respect and trust evolve.[4]

What does this mean for you as a beginning or experienced teacher? Are you comfortable with this idea? Should all teachers behave in such fashion? Why or why not? What other alternatives are there? What are the key elements involved in this open view of self?

Trust is clearly one of the key elements in freely sharing yourself in the classroom according to Carl Rogers:

> But underlying all of these behaviors is the trust he feels in the capacity of the group to develop the human potential which exists in that group and its separate members. This trust is something which cannot be faked. It is not a technique. The facilitator can only be as trusting as he in fact is. Thus he may be able to trust and give freedom in a very restricted area in which he is not risking much. But if it is real and complete, even in a narrow area, it will have a facilitating effect upon the process of the group.[5]

We also see the impact of efforts to "act like teachers" when teachers are unwilling to release some of the time-honored power that has

4. Reprinted with permission from *The Open Classroom*, a New York Review Book, 1969. Copyright © 1969 Herbert Kohl.

5. Carl Rogers, *Freedom to Learn*, p. 75.

been associated with the role of teacher. Despite feelings of uneasiness about the lack of opportunity for students to participate in more active, responsible decision making in the classroom, these individuals go right on making all the decisions themselves because, after all, that's how teachers are supposed to act. It is not an easy task to give up quantities of power, in fact, as Kohl points out, it is extremely "difficult to yield power and develop a sense of community with young people (or even with one's peers, for that matter)." The key again is that "the teacher should be as much himself as the pupils are themselves."[6]

Let us look at Robert Kunze, a junior-high-school social-studies teacher in an inner city school as an example. Robert appears in every way to have earned the respect and confidence of the students he works with. Part of this respect may have been gained through Robert's openness in sharing of himself as a human being, weaknesses included.

If you had been in Robert's class last week, you would have witnessed a good example of his willingness to share a crack in his own humanity, and to turn a delicate situation into a positive learning experience. It all started when Robert returned to his seventh-grade class after having been called to the office to answer an urgent telephone call. He had been gone for about ten minutes and, as he came down the hall toward his classroom, he could hear more than an average amount of noise and activity coming from his room. He was also greeted by some nonverbal communication:

6. Reprinted with permission from *The Open Classroom*, a New York Review Book, 1969. Copyright ©1969 Herbert Kohl.

a teaching colleague gave Robert that "can't you keep your class in order" look as he shut his own classroom door.

When Robert entered the room the noise level dropped only slightly; many of the students, still consumed by numerous small group confrontations, had not even noticed his return. Visibly upset, Robert reacted to the situation in a manner that contrasted with his normal and usually successful style of simply asking for the group's attention, perhaps kidding them somewhat about the situation, and then discussing with his class the important issues surrounding the incident.

Today was different, however, and before he gave any of the students a chance to quiet down or respond, Robert did some shouting of his own as he called the group together. He was angry and the strained temple muscles illustrated this fact clearly as he spoke. Even though his behavior produced nearly pin-dropping silence in the room, Robert was immediately shocked somewhat by his own behavior as he observed the nonverbal reaction of his class.

Many teachers at such a point might have moved right ahead on whatever the class topic for the day might have been, and let it go at that. Robert on the other hand believed that feelings surrounding such incidents, good or bad, need to be exposed honestly for what they are if a sense of communication in the group is to be maintained. Here is what Robert said to his class a few moments after his shouting:

I can see by the looks on your faces right now that you are a little shocked about my shouting at you. I am a little surprised myself but I was very angry when I came in that door and still am to a certain extent. I do think it was unfair for me to overreact to the situation by shouting at you before I even found out what was going on, but sometimes as human beings we respond like that for a number of reasons—some good, some bad.

I don't think my reasons were very good today but let me tell you what I think they were. You know, when I was called down to the office to take that call this morning, I was afraid something serious had happened to my family. It turned out to be a very angry merchant who claimed I had an overdue account at his store. I talked with him for over ten minutes trying to convince him that the bill was paid a long time ago and that I had the canceled check to prove it. He didn't believe me so I have to bring it down after school tonight.

Then as I was returning to the room someone said there was a lot of noise and commotion in my classroom and that I should hurry back. Mr. Johnson next door also looked quite upset about the noise and he didn't even speak to me as he shut his door as I came by.

These of course are not good reasons for someone shouting like I did but I hope they help explain at least why I behaved like that. How do you think I felt? Has that ever happened to you before or someone around you? How did you feel?. . . .

After a lengthy discussion that spun off such questions, Robert and his class calmed down together and eventually confronted the issues of the disrupted classroom in a rational fashion. Robert didn't teach his social studies lesson for the day—*or did he?*

QUESTIONS FOR ANALYSIS

1. Should all classroom teachers be expected to behave in an open fashion as the examples illustrated in this chapter? Why or why not?

2. What do you consider to be some of the major problems related to being genuine in your classroom? What are the potential rewards?

3. What are some of the cracks in your humanity and how do you feel they might actually be drawn from to support your work with learners?

4. What alternatives would you offer to those who may find it difficult or impossible to behave in the manner suggested by this author's concept of teacher?

5. What evidence of genuineness have you observed in teachers you have had the opportunity to work for or with down through the years?

6. In what ways can genuineness be revealed? How would you like it to be revealed in your work with learners?

7. How does the concept of genuineness apply to the role of student?

SELECTED REFERENCES

Borton, Terry. *Reach, Touch, and Teach.* New York: McGraw-Hill, 1970.

Dennison, George. *The Lives of Children.* New York: Random House, 1969.

Dreikurs, Rudolf, M.D., Grunwald, Bernice Bronia, and Pepper, Floy C. *Maintaining Sanity in the Classroom: Illustrated Teaching Techniques.* New York: Harper and Row, 1971.

Ginott, Haim G., M.D. *Between Parent and Child.* New York: Macmillan, 1968.

———. *Between Parent and Teenager.* New York: Macmillan, 1969.

Greenberg, Herbert M. *Teaching With Feeling.* New York: Pegasus, 1969.

Harris, Thomas A., M.D. *I'm OK—You're OK.* New York: Harper and Row, 1969.

Henderson, George, and Bibens, Robert F. *Teachers Should Care: Social Perspectives of Teaching.* New York: Harper and Row, 1970.

Jersild, Arthur T. *When Teachers Face Themselves.* New York: Teachers College, Columbia University, 1955.

Kohl, Herbert R. *The Open Classroom: A Practical Guide to a New Way of Teaching.* New York: Vintage Books, 1969.

Kozol, Jonathan. *Death at an Early Age.* Boston: Houghton Mifflin, 1967.

Rogers, Carl R. *Freedom to Learn.* Columbus, Ohio: Charles E. Merrill, 1969.

Shumsky, Abraham. *In Search of Teaching Style.* New York: Appleton-Century Crofts, 1968.

92

THE
TEACHER:
A Mediator

To mediate is to be instrumental in another person's experiencing of his world and in his search for meaning.[1]

1. Alice Miel, ed., *Creativity in Teaching* (Belmont, California: Wadsworth, 1961), p. 4.

These well-chosen worlds point to another key dimension of my concept of teacher—the mediating role. This dimension more than any other is the quality or characteristic that should allow the child's frame of reference to be the basic springboard to educational activity. That is, if we really believe that what a child learns in school should have immediate relevance in his life space, then one of the critical tasks of a teacher is to mediate between his world, his problems, and his concerns, and his search for meaning in that world. This process in the long run, as a matter of fact, should define school activity.

How does a teacher mediate or become instrumental in another person's experiencing of his world? It could happen in many ways.

It might occur when a teacher declares a moratorium on all other preplanned school activities to allow the children to respond, explore, or react in some meaningful way to a national event that has occurred (space flight, election, death of nationally known personality, etc.). Depending upon the nature of the happening and the interest of the learner(s), the teacher should have many opportunities to mediate between significant learnings and the event, as the group or individual pursues meaning within his life space.

A teacher may mediate simply by raising more "why" type questions in his work with learners in an attempt to draw meaningful relationships between the learners' world and school activity. Why bother to study historical events that have occurred so long ago? What effect do they have on our lives today? Responding to and instructionally taking advantage of events like a birth in the family of one of the students, a death in the family, a broken arm, an honor or award, a fight on the playground, the menu for the week's lunch program, a leak in the school roof, or any number of other major and minor occurrences provide teachers with numerous opportunities for mediating between the goals and objectives of education and the real world of the learner.

One of the keys to the teacher's mediating function is to create settings and situations where the learner feels comfortable about, and motivated to, expose his world of problems and concerns. Once these problems are verbally or nonverbally exposed, the teacher's role becomes that of assessing their potential for learning activities, for experiences that will assist the learner in his process of "becoming," and allowing the learner to participate in making decisions about his own education.

This role has not always been easy to actualize because tradition, pressures, and the fear of the unknown have been impressive obstacles for teachers to overcome in both thinking and practice. For example, teachers who are motivated to build more of the instructional program around the expressed needs and interests of children are usually bombarded by questions and comments like:

"Children don't really know what is best for them, they are too young and haven't had any real experiences with life and what it's all about."

"How are you going to make sure that the children learn all of the basics?"

"If you let children decide on what they should learn—who needs teachers?"

"Why should children have to waste all that time in trying to make decisions about what to study when that's already been done for us in the book?"

"It takes too long, and is much more confusing than just simply telling them what we are going to study."

"How can you possibly plan ahead if you keep allowing children with all their different ideas to participate in decision making?"

"My job is to teach, the child's job is to learn"

Most of these questions and concerns, of course, miss the point or are based on lack of information about children and how they learn. Children are experiencing life each and every day, but not from the adult frame of reference. It is amazing how much they do know about their needs, if only given an opportunity to express them. It is equally amazing how many basics are naturally related to the needs of children as expressed by them. The question, who needs teachers, might be rephrased to read, in what role do we need teachers? Is taking additional time to allow children to engage in the challenges and admittedly frustrating task of decision making a waste of time? Can and should students teach and teachers learn?

Yes, to be a mediator is a challenging task; as professional educators, from our own frame of reference we appear to know a great deal about our exposition role and very little about our mediating role in relationship to the child's frame of reference. In order to explore that role in greater depth I would like to offer a series of classroom episodes that show the teacher as mediator and the child as the basic decision maker. It is within this "story" about an experimental study with primary children that I hope to illustrate the numerous possibilities which exist for a teacher to mediate between the learner's real world and his quest for understanding, managing, and giving meaning to that world. I shall provide a title for my story:

"THE CHILD'S FRAME OF REFERENCE: WHY NOT?"[2]

What would happen if a primary social-studies program were to revolve exclusively around the expressed interests of children? Would the child's frame of reference be adequate? Could these interests and concerns lead to the development of what is regarded as important skills, attitudes, and understandings in social-studies education at this level? What might be omitted that is normally covered in primary social-studies programs with clearly identified scope and sequence patterns? Do in fact the expressed interests and preferences of children lie close to their actual needs as suggested by George Dennison in his stimulating analysis, *The Lives of Children*?[3]

In an attempt to explore such questions in greater depth this writer, four primary teaching colleagues,[4] and several elementary education interns conducted an action-research project revolving around student-initiated learning experiences. The purpose of this brief "story" will be to reflect on

2. This article, slightly modified, appeared in the Spring 1971 *Bulletin of the Minnesota Council For The Social Studies.*

3. George Dennison, *The Lives of Children* (New York: Vintage Books, 1969).

4. Mary Phillips, Florence Rossman, Del Faye Syverud, and Beverly Timmers, all members of the primary unit at the Campus Laboratory School at St. Cloud State College, provided the major portion of the instruction in the project described in this article.

the basic nature of this project and to speculate on its implications for the teacher's role as mediator.

Project Focus

The experimental project had its inception at a primary team planning session where the social-studies program was being discussed. Operating in a nongraded team-teaching organizational pattern, the teachers and interns seemed quite concerned about building more of the instructional program around the expressed interests of children and exploring the implications that this change had for existing social-studies activities in the primary unit. The general feeling seemed to be that as teachers we knew a great deal about structured social-studies programs and teacher-initiated school experiences and, on the other hand, very little about a more open environment where instructional leads are taken primarily from children and the teacher serves basically as mediator. For this reason we agreed to involve ourselves in some experimental work with primary children in the unit. Specifically our goals were: (1) to pursue a series of school activities that were exclusively motivated by the interests of the student, (2) to gather data about such emerging activities by way of film, video tapes, audio tape and written materials, and (3) to analyze the data gathered as related to the basic questions posed in the first paragraph of this article.

Several agreements and decisions were reached prior to initiating the project. Among the more significant of these agreements were:

1. We would involve all 75 children in the primary unit, ages five, six, and seven.

2. We would set aside a block of time, usually the first hour and a half of the school day, within which project activities could emerge. This would replace the regular social-studies program for the duration of the project.

3. We would only pursue topics and activities that, as closely as we would be able to determine, were of genuine interest to the children.

4. We would purposely exaggerate the teacher's role as mediator in an attempt to maximize opportunities to be directed by student decisions and interests. We realize that the temptations to steer and dominate activities by teacher decisions would be numerous and in many cases perhaps justified. To allow that to happen, however, would work contrary to our goal of seeing where student interests and their decisions about them might lead us in the development of skills, attitudes, and understandings which would be educationally sound and relevant for these children.

5. We would audio tape as many of our team planning sessions as possible throughout the project, and we would video tape, film, and provide written accounts of as many aspects of the actual work with children as could be arranged. This descriptive data of our work would be used later for the purpose of analysis.

Our Starting Place, the Playground

To find our starting place the teachers were asked to name the children's major topics of conversation—before the start of the actual school day, during the noon hour, and/or after school—the kind of topics in other words, which are all too frequently cut off from the mainstream of school activity by the following typical comment which might start the school day, "OK children, let's stop that chattering now and settle down; school is ready to start." One often wonders what educational opportunities are lost by cutting off spontaneous activity and separating it from "what we are supposed to do at school."

It was within these "outside of school" discussions where we found what we considered to be an appropriate starting place for our project: the school playground and related activity. According to the teachers, this seemed to be the source of most conversation ranging from chatter about games, fights, and chasing butterflies to comments about friends and foes on the playground. Our starting point might have been a state or national event, a moon trip or a major snowmobile race. It might have been the weather, or the birth of a new baby into one of the youngster's families. It might have been a new student in the school or a new cast on the arm of one of the children who had recently had an accident. It might even have been the new building being constructed across the street. Indeed, the interest and concern might have been generated from any number of possible sources. The important point was that it was of natural interest and concern to the children. In this case it happened to be the playground.

Our first mediating task was that of opening up the educational environment to allow such discussions to occur "on school time." And so it was that plans were made to allow for a continuation of discussion revolving around the playground on a Monday morning. Seated informally on the carpet and casual furniture the students, teacher, and interns took the first step forward in our experimental project. The teachers offered a few general questions to start and encourage the conversation and the plan was for the student's comments to provide direction for us from there.

Our first major surprise came only moments later when we were greated by such comments as, "Our playground is a lovely place, We have slides and teeter-totters on our playground, We have fun on our playground," etc. This wasn't at all the way the conversations sounded in the halls. Why had the tone changed so dramatically? It was as though the children were saying, in some conditioned response fashion, This is what you want to hear, isn't it? From a teacher's standpoint, I can recall my feelings of inner pain as these first few comments were offered. Can school really be so separated from the real world of children? There is no doubt in my mind that this question needs the immediate attention of educators at all levels.

Resisting the temptation to steer the group in directions where their interests were not naturally leading them, the teachers in this setting continued simply to mediate between the variables of what they had sensed to be a real interest on the part of the children and the element of time. We simply didn't rush the children but rather encouraged them to continue to share their ideas no matter how conditioned their responses appeared to be. An interesting thing happened. The longer they talked about the playground, the more natural their comments appeared to be. "We never have a chance to finish our games." "Tommy always gets to use the play horse." "There are not enough balls to play with." "Jane and I like to play with the boys but they never let us." "There is nothing to do on the playground." Many reactions were offered and a number of personal confrontations, individual and group, took place in the ensuing discussion. In fact one young lad who had apparently assumed the role of "king of the playground" was challenged by a number of children. The real world of the playground began to appear.

Now we were feeling much closer to our original goal of starting with some genuine concerns of children. But where would we go from here? True to our original plan only the children would really be able to answer this with the teacher, again as planned, serving basically as mediator. Appropriate to this role were the following teacher statements and questions which were raised in the discussion, "My, you really have a lot of interesting things to say about your playground. I didn't know you felt that way about many things. You have some good things to say and some bad." These comments, and others, led up to what I would consider to be a key mediating question, "With all of the problems you say you have on the playground, is there anything that you would like to do to change your playground and maybe make it a better place?" Note that the teacher has not told the children what to do but rather has raised a question which in this case is aimed at mediating between a series of expressed problems of children and the opportunity to attempt to solve some of them. We were prepared to honor a yes or no type response to this question.

The children's response to the situation was affirmative and they did want to do something about their playground. In all honesty, however, through nonverbal reaction some of the children in the group suggested that they really didn't believe we would seriously let them do anything about it. Their response seemed to suggest that the teachers probably had some new piece of playground equipment in the back room in a crate; at best, their job was to guess what it was.

Time again appeared to be an important factor, for the longer we discussed this matter the more convinced the children seemed to be that we really were serious and they in fact could follow through on plans to change their playground. As might be expected, the ideas about how to make our playground a better place varied greatly. The following is a representative sampling of the suggestions:

We could build a playhouse on our playground.

We could get some old trees to climb on.

We could dig some tunnels on our playground.

We should get some more nice people for our playground.

We should have a golden teeter-totter on our playground.

We could build a swimming pool on our playground.

We should have live horses on our playground to ride.

We could get a rubber seat for our swing.

We could plant a garden and trees on our playground.

As these suggestions and others were offered by the children it was very difficult to maintain our mediating role. For example, the teachers had to overcome the temptation to say that swimming pools and live horses were out of the question because of their size, cost, and other factors. And it wasn't easy. On the other hand, we also had to curtail the temptation to get overly excited about suggestions like a rubber seat on the swing, which seemed to be so possible and therefore such a "good" idea. Again it might have been appropriate to provide more teacher direction in such an activity at this point, but our goal was to provide children with the opportunity to steer our course of action so we resisted the temptation.

Even though the project was barely off the ground at this point several "social studies" type concerns and problems began to emerge such as:

The obvious confrontations with the most basic of all economic principles, unlimited wants vs. limited resources.

The opportunity to comment on aspects of the immediate environment and to consider possible ways and means of bringing about needed change in that environment.

To be faced with the problem of establishing priorities since we couldn't do everything we wanted to.

To define problems and identify questions relating to these problems that are important to producing a solution.

To appreciate the wide variety of interest of a large number of peers and to make plans which take into consideration these varied interests.

We Mobilize for Action

The next major phase of the project was the establishment of interest groups to actually follow through on many of the areas and recommendations that had been suggested to improve the playground. All of the areas were posted on bulletin boards throughout the primary unit and the children were asked to sign up for any group they were interested in. Several groups of varying sizes were established from this activity among them:

1. A group to explore the possibility of building a playhouse for the playground.

2. A group to explore the possibility of building tunnels.

3. A group to explore having live horses on the playground.

4. A group to explore planting trees and shrubs.

5. A group to explore planting a garden.

6. A group to explore painting equipment on the playground.

7. A group to explore having a swimming pool on our playground.

It will not be possible to discuss the major follow-through activities for each of these groups. Space does not allow. Therefore, only the major activities of the "live horses" committee will be presented. Hopefully this will suffice as a representative sample of the overall nature of the project at this level.

Live Horses on the Playground

When the children first suggested live horses on the playground I must admit that I felt their pursuit of this goal would be brief, fruitless, and if you will pardon me, a "dead horse issue" which would not lead the group in the direction of major social-studies learning experiences. This was not the first time I have been wrong on such matters. Let me explain.

When we came together for our first planning meeting (eight children and teacher), the children seemed very confident that live horses would certainly make our playground a better place, and there would be no problem at all in arranging this. All we had to do was buy some horses and build a fence and we would be all set. It all seemed so easy and so exciting and the children jumped from one dream to another as they described what it would be like.

It was at this point where a rather strong temptation began to emerge once again to intervene and protect the children from what appeared to be some rather certain future disappointments.

Because of the nature of the experimental project it was decided to allow the project on horses to go its natural course following the leads of children and not providing a cushion for some of the bumps that might lie ahead. Actually I believe we provide too many cushions for children in our school programs and rob them of opportunities to be disappointed and unhappy and to begin at early levels to deal with these emotions in an open and healthy fashion. As a matter of fact it would seem that such a situation might qualify as a major social-studies experience of the highest order in the affective domain.

As the planning session continued the children brought themselves back to reality with questions like:

Where will we get the money?

Who will feed the horses?

What will we do with them at night?

What will we do with them in the winter?

Who will clean up after the horses? etc.

One child seemed to be inquiring about our seriousness in this whole matter and provided a next step, when he asked, "Well, if we really are going to do it, I suppose we will have to get permission first." Everyone agreed that this was a good idea and that the principal would be the person to ask for such permission.

The next day we arranged to have lunch with the principal to ask him about our idea. After meeting with him for a half hour the children discovered that it was not completely up to him whether or not we could have a horse on the playground. He provided us with some help and ideas; also, we came up with many new questions and problems. As far as social studies is concerned, it might be interesting to point out that we were learning many new things about our principal without the principal being the object of study. We didn't learn all there was to know about our principal but then this might not be the last interest or problem that would lead us to him again in the future. Is there a difference between learning about the principal and studying the principal?

After our meeting with the principal we talked about who else we might ask for permission. Child logic provided us with the next step, when one child said, "Well, I don't know who can give us permission, but I know who would tell us to take a horse off the playground if it was not supposed to be there—a policeman." And so our next step was to talk to the policeman. The next day arrangements were made to visit the police station.

Our meeting with the policeman provided us with the first major disappointment when he said, "No, you cannot have live horses on your playground all the time." He explained the reasons why. We then came up with a new option that provided everyone, myself included (for by this time the children had convinced me that it was not such a wild idea as I had originally thought), with a new ray of hope for our project. Perhaps we could bring in a horse one day a month. The police department agreed to go along with this but said we needed to check with the health department. The policeman gave us the names and addresses of city health department officials and the names of people who might have horses they might be willing to bring to our playground for such one-day affairs, if we could get the approval and make the necessary arrangements. Part of the smiles began to appear on the children's faces once again as we left the police department. We had adjusted our plans because of new information and again I ask you, Is this not a part of social-studies goals and objectives? And what did we learn about the policeman, again without the policeman being the object of study? What other natural interests and problems might lead us to him in the future?

As the project moved forward, several other natural social-studies experiences emerged. For example:

We visited the health department, received their permission, and learned about the health department in the process.

We learned more about simple maps as we located places in the community we needed to visit.

We read about horses in books as we planned our work.

We learned some things about newspapers as we looked for horses for sale in the paper. We didn't try to force learning beyond our present needs because we felt new needs would provide future opportunities to learn more about the newspaper.

We had older children in the school help us with some of our work because some of them owned horses and had available information to share with us.

We visited a horse farm and the owner was convinced by the children to bring some horses into the school. Certain conditions would need to be met for safety, supervision, and other matters; all of these were within reason for the school. The fact that the school year ended was the only reason that the "live horses" did not arrive on the playground. But, then, why not next year? The children will be back.

These are only a representative sampling of the experiences that emerged from one group of children. If space would allow, similar stories might be shared of the other groups.

The playhouse group, for example, did build a playhouse for the playground. They worked with the shop teacher and found money in the school budget for supplies. They planned how large they would make it, how it would be used, and what materials they would need (the type of paint, etc.). In the process the concept of division of labor became obvious to the children without it being mentioned once to my knowledge. Did it need to be?

The garden group followed through by actually planting a garden on the playground. They had to concern themselves with what to plant, when to plant, how to plant. They used moms, dads, and grandparents as helpers. Once again we might ask, How important is it for children in social programs to have the opportunity to interact with adults in meaningful ways on real problems and issues?

What about the tree group where one child couldn't understand why we were going to plant trees if we couldn't actually see them grow up, and another child responded, "Well we aren't just doing this for ourselves, we are doing it for all the people who will be in our school even when we are not here." What springboards for social-studies learnings could be related to this situation?

Looking Back and Looking Ahead

First impressions seem to indicate that the children have indeed led us in pursuit of significant social-studies goals as commonly expressed. The material gathered gives every indication that during this period of time we maintained a sharp focus on man and his relationship to himself, to other men, and to the physical and psychological worlds that surround him. We seem to have touched down on all of the social-science areas in one way or another, some extensively and others in more limited fashion. We have also been steered naturally to many other fields such as math, science, art, etc., all within the surrounding community. Admittedly we only scratched the surface in our experimental work. The original question, however, was raised with less hesitation all the time—*the child's frame of reference: why not?*

QUESTIONS FOR ANALYSIS

1. How will you, or do you, mediate in the world of children?

2. Are there problems and concerns in the world of learners that are *not* the business of the school and its goals? If so, what type of problems and concerns are they and how will you deal with them if they are exposed to you as a teacher?

3. How will you, or do you, create settings and situations where learners feel comfortable and motivated to share problems and concerns related to their world? What are some of the existing elements which appear to stand in the way?

4. What are the "basics" that we hear so much about in discussions on school practice? What do you consider "basics" in your work with children?

5. What examples can you recall in your own education where a teacher assisted you or your fellow students in creating study opportunities around a genuinely expressed interest of yours? What do you remember most about these experiences?

6. How would you react to the statement, "My job is to teach, the child's job is to learn"?

7. Herbert Kohl in *Open Classroom* states that "the teacher is a mediator and not a judge or executioner."[5] What does this statement mean to you and what are the implications for your work with children?

8. As you critique the "story" shared in this chapter, what are some of the major concerns that come to mind? Did the interests of children lead to "basics"? Can we count on open classroom examples such as this to lead to all of the concerns of the school? How would you change or modify the teachers' behavior as illustrated? Why?

SELECTED REFERENCES

Borton, Terry. *Reach, Touch, and Teach.* New York: McGraw-Hill, 1970.

Dennison, George. *The Lives of Children.* New York: Random House, 1969.

Holt, John. *The Underachieving School.* New York: Pitman, 1969.

———. *How Children Fail.* New York: Pitman, 1964.

———. *How Children Learn.* New York: Pitman, 1969.

———. *What Do I Do Monday?* New York: Dutton, 1970.

Kohl, Herbert R. *The Open Classroom: A Practical Guide to a New Way of Teaching.* New York: Vintage Books, 1969.

Miel, Alice, ed. *Creativity in Teaching.* Belmont, California: Wadsworth, 1961.

Neill, A. A. *Summerhill.* New York: Hart, 1960.

5. Reprinted with permission from *The Open Classroom*, A New York Review Book, 1969. Copyright © 1969 Herbert Kohl.

106

THE
TEACHER:
On Motivation

A teacher affects eternity; he can never tell where his influence stops.

Henry Adams

Alan Pirez is thirteen years old and lives with his mother and five brothers and sisters in a small two-bedroom apartment in the heart of a large city. Alan attends a large and overcrowded junior high school near his home and has a rather remarkable attendance record in that he rarely misses school. There may be a number of reasons for Alan's interest in being in school but, if you asked Mrs. Pirez, she would cite Alan's social-studies teacher Mr. Glen Worthington as the key factor. "Mr. Worthington really cares about Alan and Alan knows it. He is the kind of teacher that most kids want to work with and he really makes school interesting. *He really motivates his students.*" Does Glen Worthington really motivate his students? Is it possible for one human being to motivate another? What in fact is motivation and how does it relate to the world of teaching?

What mental image have you formed of Glen Worthington based on Mrs. Pirez's remarks? Do you see him as a dynamic, outgoing personality? Do you see him as a soft-spoken, warm, nurturing-type individual? Does he have a staccato style? Is he young, old, graying, bald, muscle-bound, tall, slightly built, flashily dressed, conservative? Is he verbal? Does he surround himself with exciting teaching media and hardware? Does he have a wide range of interests? Does he teach from a book? Does he divide the class into small discussion groups rather than keep the large group with lecture as the mode of instruction? Does he use a number of teaching gimmicks in his work with young people? Does he smile a lot? Does he have a low-pitched even voice which is pleasant to listen to? Are there in fact characteristics that distinguish high-quality from low-quality teachers in the world of "motivation"?

Consider the following classroom episodes:

Mary Johnson, third-grade teacher, has just asked the students to shut their eyes and mentally record all of the sounds they hear around them. This is the first experience in a unit on sound and Mary intends to build on this activity through discussion as the class moves forward in their exploration of this area.

"How far will I be able to blow the pingpong ball out of the large end of this funnel?" is a question that Jim Roberts, junior-high-school science teacher, asks as he launches a class discussion on air pressure. He expects a wide variation of guesses and speculations that will assist him in getting at critical issues with his class when he actually attempts to blow the pingpong ball out—and, of course, it remains in the funnel.

A senior-high-school history class breaks into laughter as their teacher enters the room dressed in a historical costume that relates to a historical figure they are actually studying. The teacher assumes the character of the individual and proceeds to discuss many issues through the historical character's frame of reference.

Pollution is the focal point of study for a fifth-grade class who have just been told by their teacher that they will be leaving on a walk through the community to look for local problems and areas of concern related to their topic of study. The class appears excited as they put on their coats and eagerly line up at the door.

A junior-high-school teacher leans over and quietly speaks to one of her English students, "Mary, your story is really quite good and I think, if you are willing, it should be shared with others. I was wondering if you might be interested in going with me next week when I plan to visit one of the elementary schools to do some story telling. I am sure they would enjoy hearing your story.

A live telecast of a moon walk is just turned off by Charles Hathoway, senior-high-school current-affairs instructor, as he poses the following questions to his class, "What are your reactions to what you have just observed? What is the significance of this event for man?"

An intermediate teacher has turned off all the lights in a small room and has just lit a candle. Fifteen sets of eyes focus on the candle and the teacher's face as he starts his "gory" story about ancient medical practice and discussion of the concept of change in attitude and practice as it relates to growth in the medical profession.

"Look at this interesting sugar beet that Tom has brought in. He says you can really make sugar from it. Do you think we can? How many would like to try?" This item for Show and Tell has propelled Sally Olson and her class into an unplanned activity. And away they go.

"What kind of feelings do you have about the girl in this film?" is the first question raised by Mr. Peterson as he launches a discussion about a film the class has just viewed in his senior-high-school social-studies class.

It is late at night and Helen Olson has just put the finishing touches on her current-issues classroom. She expects to meet her class for the first time tomorrow and she has "filled" every bit of space in her room with books, pamphlets, films, filmstrips, newspapers, magazines, and many other items which point to various contemporary issues. She plans to remain silent unless called upon as her students come into the room and begin interacting with this environment.

"That's a good idea, Tom. If you can get that information from your dad about the cost of lumber in his yard, we will be able to use it in our planning. Why don't you try to get it for us by tomorrow?"

A teacher smiles and nods in an acknowledging way to Mike who has just nonverbally reacted to something he has silently read during a study period.

Which of these episodes reflects the highest levels of motivation for the individuals involved? Can you tell? Is it possible to tell from the information given? Obviously not, and it is hoped that the following frame of reference will help explain why.

Motivation, a Frame of Reference

I do not intend at this point to explore in great depth the concept of motivation as it relates to the world of classroom teaching. The literature abounds with in-depth explorations of this topic and therefore the goal in this area will remain as it has been for other issues explored—simply to point out key elements as related to my concept of teacher. We begin with the question, Do teachers motivate students to learn? My answer is no. A teacher or any other human being is incapable of motivating another individual. As Avila, Combs, and Purkey point out, "there is only one kind of motivation, and that is the personal, internal motivation that each and every human being has at all times, in all places, and when engaged in any activity."[1] As teachers we therefore cannot motivate students to learn, but we can control and modify an environment of human and material resources in such ways as to provide situations which have the potential of being personally meaningful and enhancing to the student.

Combs provides perhaps the best framework for this position when he states:

> People are *always* motivated if they are forever engaged in seeking self-fulfillment. Indeed, they are never unmotivated unless they are dead. To be sure, they may not be motivated to do what some outsider believes they ought or should. The little boy in school who pokes the pretty little girl in front of him during the arithmetic lesson is not very motivated at that moment to do arithmetic, but he is surely not unmotivated! In the light of our discussion of the growth principle, motivation is not a problem of external manipulations; it has to do with what goes on inside people. It is always there, "given" by the very nature of the life force itself.[2]

This, of course, is the reason why we couldn't evaluate the teaching episodes cited earlier in this chapter. All we had the opportunity to note was external factors; the crucial factors related to the child's level of motivations were not visible. This is not to say that the situations described in each of the episodes were not personally meaningful to the students involved. They all had that potential, but no one can determine how meaningful an experience is by knowing only the nature of the activity itself.

1. Donald L. Avila, Arthur W. Combs, and William W. Purkey, *The Helping Relationship Sourcebook* (Boston: Allyn and Bacon, 1971), p. 114.

2. Arthur W. Combs, Donald L. Avila, and William W. Purkey, *Helping Relationships: Basic Concepts for the Helping Professions* (Boston: Allyn and Bacon, 1971), p. 76.

It is unfortunate that we have in the past made such an issue of intrinsic vs. extrinsic motivation. As Avila, Combs, and Purkey point out it is a regrettable distinction.[3] Because of this we have tended to focus most of our attention as educators on extrinsic motivational techniques to the point where we have obscured the true nature of motivation. It has prevented us from "becoming highly skilled in the process that is truly the essence of all human interaction, that is, controlled manipulation."[4] This controlled manipulation is simply the process by which, as teacher, you manipulate yourself and other classroom variables in such a way that what you are trying to teach appears to be self-enhancing to the students.

Frymier and Thompson help crystalize this concept of motivation as it relates to education:

> This picture of motivation suggests that motivation to learn in school is something which students *have* or *are* rather than that which teachers *do* to help them learn. Studies now under way suggest that motivation to learn in school is a fairly *constant* factor. It is subject to change, but generally only slowly. Teachers *can* affect students' motivational levels, but over extended periods of time like a year; probably very little in a single day.

> Motivation to learn in school is a function of one's personality structure, his goals and values, his conception of self and others, and his attitude toward change. These aspects of human behavior are learned and they are subject to modification. Nevertheless, teachers concerned about their youngster's motivations have to do much more than use a carrot on a stick or a paddle on the behind if they hope for significant changes in any way.[5]

Our basic task as teachers therefore is not to motivate students but rather to create educational situations, experiences, and settings where personal motives can be extended and enhanced. Let us apply this to the classroom.

Motivation Facilitated

With the view of motivation taken by this author, it should be clear at this point that the role of the teacher in using rewards and punish-

3. Donald L. Avila, Arthur W. Combs, and William W. Purkey, *The Helping Relationship Sourcebook* (Boston: Allyn and Bacon, 1971), p. 113.

4. Ibid., p. 114.

5. J. R. Frymier and J. H. Thompson, "Motivation: The Learner's Mainspring," *Educational Leadership* 22 (1965): 567-70.

ments to make students learn relevant material is out of focus. Rather the teacher's role is seen to be that of facilitator, helping students to:

relate to the world around them through their own natural motives to understand that world,

discover and explore new goals and values,

raise questions about themselves and their relationships to the world at all levels,

modify their existing motivational levels over periods of time,

become more sophisticated in understanding their motives in life and to become more skilled and knowledgeable in pursuing them.

It is not enough for the teacher to say or to imply that what we are studying is important; that we will need it for success in life, for the next level of education or, for that matter, even for the here and now which we have already commented on as the learner's most significant frame of reference. The key as teacher is to become skilled in what we have referred to as "controlled manipulation." Through control of ourselves and the environment, our goal is for the student to say for himself, *"This is important to me."* The students' motives are personal and all we can hope to do is to facilitate them in establishing a solid relationship to the world about them. Let us examine a classroom example.

Why Study Explorers?

Jack Carlson has always been concerned about students' interest or lack of it in studying about historical events. Do students really understand why they are studying such events or people? Should we be spending as much time on history as we do in our schools? Is there such a thing as natural motivation for such study and, if so, how does the teacher manipulate himself and the environment in such a way as to facilitate and enhance the learners' pursuit of these motives? The following is a brief commentary on Jack's attempt in a fifth-grade unit of study on early explorers.

As a starter Jack went before his class and asked for the use of their imagination. He told the class that he was in fact a stranger from another planet and that he was just learning the English language. One of the words that he was trying to learn about was the word "explorer," and as he wrote it on the board he asked his class if they would please explain it to him. What is the word? What can you tell me about it? What does it mean?

The students responded immediately and it wasn't long before a series of examples was offered relating to past explorers (Columbus, Vikings, etc.), to modern explorers (space, oceanographers, etc.) and even to the children themselves as explorers (of the neighborhood, beach, new home, etc.). The fact that the children regarded themselves as explorers was, for Jack, a significant development and if they hadn't come up with the idea he would have offered himself (controlled manipulation) as an explorer, in order to provide a more personal bridge in his facilitating efforts.

Jack's next questions were, Why do people explore? What are the major reasons? Here the children bounced back and forth from their frame of reference as explorers to what they sensed to be the frame of reference of other historical or modern explorers. They offered as reasons that people explore: enjoyment, food, needs of man, curiosity, to make lives easier, to make a living, etc.

At this point Jack began to aim more precisely at the child's frame of reference as he asked, Why do you explore? How do you feel? Do you think it takes special qualities to be an explorer? If so, what kind of qualities?

After some discussion on this point the group was faced with a serious question. We can speak for ourselves, but how can we react for those who lived long ago or even for the modern explorers whom we cannot ask directly (astronaut)? How could Jack as teacher meet this concern by controlled manipulation?

His reaction to the situation was to plan a specific activity, a simulated experience which the class might build on. He visited a local science center where he acquired a real space helmet and the latest "Apollo 7" films and in the middle of his classroom he simulated an Apollo flight with the use of the film and other equipment. The experience provided a natural springboard for several significant questions. As someone "inside the helmet," how do you think you'd feel? What kind of things would you need to know? What kind of qualities should you have? Why would you want to go? What dangers exist? What rewards?

The next set of questions the group began to explore was, Is it more difficult to explore in modern times or in the past? Did explorers of the past need the same qualities as today's explorers? Were the explorer's problems different? Were the rewards the same?

For Jack it was obvious that the bridge was beginning to form. Through his leadership the children had the opportunity to link their natural motives in the area of exploration with a created situation in the classroom. They had come by way of the modern explorer but they were also looking back and, most important, *asking questions.*

Before their study was over they had examined and analyzed many historical explorations, events, and people and, perhaps even more important, they had squarely confronted the question, Why do we study about things in the past? Their responses to this question were: for appreciation, for keeping the memory of man, because it's interesting, we learn from mistakes, to be more sophisticated about the concept of change, etc. Although some educators may debate the meaning of these responses, in this experience they were a natural bridge between student motives and school experiences.

114   Variables of Teacher Control

What variables can we control in our attempt to develop natural bridges between school experiences and natural motives of the learners? Perhaps the best response to this question comes in Madeline Hunter's concise and to-the-point book *Motivation*,[6] which is part of her theory-into-practice series. In this practical approach to translating significant learning theory into meaningful classroom application, Dr. Hunter discusses potential teacher control of the variables of interest, feeling, tone (positive, negative, and neutral), reward, concern and tension, success, knowledge of results, and intrinsic-extrinsic motivation. In each of these areas Dr. Hunter, through the use of classroom examples and a programmed format for active reader responses, clearly demonstrates controlled manipulation in its most ideal sense. Her book is hightly recommended reading for those who wish to pursue motivation theory as applied to the teacher.

QUESTIONS FOR ANALYSIS

1. What do you feel are the values, if any, in making distinctions between intrinsic vs. extrinsic motivation?

2. What do you consider to be some of the major concerns that surround the concept of motivation shared by this author in this chapter?

3. Do you believe that all human relationships are controlled and manipulated? What are the implications for your role as teacher if you believe this? How might this concept be misunderstood?

6. Madeline Hunter, *Motivation* (El Segundo, California: Tip Publications, 1971).

4. What examples can you cite of controlled manipulation in your background of experiences as related to schools and classrooms?

5. Do you feel that grades should ever be considered an important motivating factor for learning? Why or why not?

SELECTED REFERENCES

Avila, Donald L., Combs, Arthur W., and Purkey, William W. *The Helping Relationship Sourcebook*. Boston: Allyn and Bacon, 1971.

Baller, Warren R., and Charles, Don C. *The Psychology of Human Growth and Development*. New York: Holt, Rinehart and Winston, 1961.

Combs, Arthur W., Avila, Donald L., and Purkey, William W. *Helping Relationships: Basic Concepts for the Helping Professions*. Boston: Allyn and Bacon, 1971.

Hall, J. F. *Psychology of Motivation*. Philadelphia: J. B. Lippincott, 1961.

Hunter, Madeline. *Motivation*. El Segundo, California: Tip Publications, 1971.

Jersild, Arthur T. *Child Psychology*. Englewood Cliffs, New Jersey: Prentice-Hall, 1968.

Kuethe, James L. *The Teaching-Learning Process*. Glenview, Ill.: Scott, Foresman, 1968.

Morrison, A., and McIntyre, D. *Teachers and Teaching*. Baltimore, Maryland: Penguin, 1969.

Ohles, John F. *Introduction to Teaching*. New York: Random House, 1970.

Perceiving, Behaving, Becoming. Association for Supervision and Curriculum Development, Washington, D.C., 1962.

116

THE
TEACHER:
A Scholar

*The teacher who walks in the shadow of the temple,
among his followers, gives not of his wisdom, but rather of
his faith and his lovingness.*

*If he is indeed wise, he does not bid you enter
the house of his wisdom, but rather leads you to the
threshold of his own mind.*

Kahlil Gibran, *The Prophet*[1]

1. Kahlil Gibran, *The Prophet* (New York: Alfred A. Knopf, 1971).

There was a time when the statement, "I teach children not subjects," was music to my ears and a positive indication of a dimension of educational philosophy I highly endorsed. I still feel that way but I must confess that recently I have been somewhat alarmed by what I sense on occasion to be a de-emphasis of solid intellectual achievement. Our movement toward such commendable goals as child-oriented programs, humanistically based curriculums, personalized school experiences and open classrooms are not to be denied as worthwhile educational directions. The tragedy is that many regard solid intellectual achievement as the enemy in this quest. Even though it is clear beyond a shadow of a doubt that schools at all levels have held hollow, meaningless content goals for students and have packaged knowledge for distribution in ways that are not defensible, this in no way should suggest that helping to produce well-informed, intelligent, knowing individuals is still not a worthy, if not prime, goal of the school. For my concept of teacher this means in addition to those dimensions of skill, understanding, and character that I have already explored with you, a teacher should also be a scholar, that is, a well-informed and knowing individual.

118

Knowledge in Perspective

The first thing we must keep in mind when exploring the teacher's role as scholar is that the acquisition of knowledge should infrequently be a goal in and of itself. Although there are occasions when individuals satisfy certain needs through knowledge accumulation, clearly the prime motivation should arise from man's inner drive to find meaning in his life. *Knowledge acquired* is a result of earlier experiences to discover that meaning, and *knowledge sought* is part of man's on-going quest to solve problems in his life. For a teacher this means that the pursuit of knowledge, in the many areas related to pre-service and in-service growth and development, should be relevant to personal and professional goals. Knowledge for knowledge's sake is a concept we have already condemned in this analysis and we should guard against the goal of "to know" overshadowing the goal of "to feel," as so eloquently expressed by A. S. Neill:

> When I lecture to students at teacher training colleges and universities, I am often shocked at the ungrownupness of these lads and lasses stuffed with useless knowledge. They know a lot; they shine in dialectics; they can quote the classics—but in their outlook on life many of them are infants. For they have been taught *to know*, but have not been allowed *to feel*. These students are friendly, pleasant, eager, but something is lacking—the emotional factor, the power to subordinate thinking to feeling. I talk to these of a world they have missed and go on missing. Their textbooks do not deal with human character, or with love, or with freedom, or with self-determination. And so the system goes on, aiming only at standards of book learning—goes on separating the head from the heart.[2]   **119**

The perspective we seek is to keep the head in close relationship to the heart for, as a number of educators have pointed out, it is possible to know without being wise. For teachers, wisdom is by far a more desirable goal.

Knowledge: Many Sources

What kind of knowledge should a teacher possess? The typical response to this question is knowledge of his subject, and rightly so. Math teachers need to know math; biology teachers need to know biology; history teachers need to know history, and so on down the line. Further, it is basic and important that a teacher have depth of knowledge in his or her area which carries them beyond what might be covered within a course of study. This means staying abreast of recent developments in one's field of study and applying his knowledge in many ways. Indeed, a teacher should be knowledgeable about his or her subject area but it is only one of many areas in which the teacher is called upon to be a scholar.

For example, in addition to being a scholar in a given field of study the teacher must also be knowledgeable about the learners with whom he or she works. At an overall level this means being knowledgeable about growth and development characteristics of the age level or levels worked with. It means knowing children, youth, or adults from physical, emotional, sociological, and psychological frames of reference. It means being knowledgeable about the learner's world of play, work, fear, questions, and many other dimensions that make up the learner's world.

2. From *Summerhill: A Radical Approach to Child Rearing*, by A. S. Neill, copyright 1960 Hart Publishing Company, New York.

At the classroom level, it also means knowing a specific group of learners—their backgrounds, their strengths, their weaknesses, their interests, etc. It means possessing knowledge about the learner's academic world, his social world, his emotional world, his family world, his friend world, his enemy world, and again all dimensions of the on-going world of a specific group of children.

The teacher must also be a scholar of instructional strategies. This means possessing and seeking knowledge about various approaches to instruction and being able to determine their appropriateness in a specific classroom setting or situation. Inquiry-oriented teaching strategies, lecturing, questioning techniques, discussion strategies, recitations, simulation, and project methods are among the many areas where teachers need a working knowledge. The literature abounds with explorations and evaluations of these strategies and it is the responsibility of the teacher to be digesting this information as it relates to his professional responsibilities in the classroom.

Another dimension where scholarship is demanded of the teacher is the philosophy of education. Why do we have schools? What are the purposes of education? Is the role of the school seen to be that of transmitting or that of an active change agent in our society? Should education be compulsory? These questions and many others relating to the theoretical underpinnings of the role of education are explored in great depth in historical and contemporary literature. Today's teacher needs to be well informed about these philosophical issues which are related to many decisions that he or she will make or participate in making.

To be a well-informed citizen in areas of government, community activities, world and national affairs and the many other general aspects of life and living is still another dimension of scholarship for today's teacher. Because so much of the life and activity of the school has, or at least should have, a direct link with the local, state, national, and international communities it is a part of, the teacher should be an informed and knowledgeable citizen. Television, newspapers, radio, and magazines simplify this task for a teacher who possesses the basic motivation.

Knowledge: a Commitment

The quality of scholarliness carries with it an on-going commitment to learning. For a teacher this means a constant craving and search for knowledge related to areas of interest and responsibility. It means for a teacher of social studies scholarly pursuits beyond the four basic years of college instruction including reading, workshops, travel, advanced professional training, etc., all aimed at the goal of being a knowing individual in his or her field.

As a knowing individual a teacher is in a much better position to respond to the wide range of needs that are likely to be a part of any group of learners he or she may work with. This is a difficult task but a basic one and one that should reap rich learning dividends. As Highet points out:

A limited field of material stirs very few imaginations. It can be learnt off by heart, but seldom creatively understood and never loved. A subject that carries the mind out in limitless journeys will, if it is well taught, make the learner eager to master all the preliminary essentials and press on.[3]

The rapid rate at which knowledge becomes outdated and obsolete is another strong reason why a teacher must maintain an on-going commitment to the study of his field or related areas of concerns. It is not enough to fill the receptacles of the mind with knowledge and, once full, to empty them. Rather, a constant sorting process must be going on so that we have available at any given point the most current and up-to-date knowledge and information that our abilities and talents will allow. It is a continuous process.

Being a knowledgeable individual within our field and beyond also holds potential for "turning on" an otherwise uninterested student. It is sometimes the teacher's eagerness and depth of understanding about a subject that spurs certain learners on.

It is true that we cannot all be fountains of energy and novelty throughout every day, but we ought, if we are teachers, to be so keen on our own subjects that we can talk interestingly about unusual aspects of them to young people who would otherwise have been dully neutral, or—worse—eager but disappointed. A teacher must believe in the value and interest of his subject as a doctor believes in health.[4]

In addition to believing in and valuing your subject area, it is also important to like your field. To like, in this instance, means having the capacity to be so interested in the area that you do not always tend to think of the subject in terms of work. It means being willing to spend extra time, even when tired, to explore the area in greater depth with the only reward being self-satisfaction. It means radiating the quality of happiness and enjoyment to others as you go about the day-to-day activity in your field.

Knowledge: a Means to an End

The fact that 55 percent of college students in America cheat to achieve higher grades is one of several indicators that should alert us to the undesirability of content or knowledge being an end in and of itself. Knowl-

3. Gilbert Highet, *The Art of Teaching* (New York: Alfred A. Knopf, 1950), p. 14.

4. Ibid., p. 14.

edge must be considered only a means to an end with the end being *knowing in light of personal and societal purposes and goals.* As Combs so clearly expresses it:

> Content must be meaningful; it is not an end in itself. It is not enough to produce teachers who *collect* facts. We must find ways of producing teachers who *find meaning in* facts and who help their students to do so. There are limits to what any teacher can or should know. Whether we like it or not, we shall often have to be content with having our children taught by teachers who do not know all about the subject. The good teacher's task is to stimulate and facilitate learning. The measure of his success is not the degree to which his students are like him, but the degree to which he has assisted his students to transcend him.[5]

As teacher-scholars we need to keep this point sharply in focus, in our own quest for knowledge and also in our leadership efforts, as we attempt to help learners find meaning in their lives. It is a difficult task because so much knowledge surrounds us. Our goal is not to know all there is to know, but rather to develop a *professional rhythm* of scholarliness that will offer continuous knowledge support for problems and concerns that are vital to us and our work. *And the beat goes on.*

QUESTIONS FOR ANALYSIS

1. What experiences have you had in which knowledge for its own sake has been illustrated? How will you be able to avoid similar occurrences in your work as teachers? Should all such occurrences be avoided?

2. Describe as concisely as possible what you as an individual know about local, state, national, and international events? Do you or would you feel comfortable discussing the political situation in a classroom setting? If not, what could you do to become better informed about this subject?

3. Have you established a professional rhythm for "knowing" in your fields of concentration? Can you describe it?

4. How do you evaluate your professional training and background to date as related to the concept of scholarliness? How are you working toward refining and extending strengths you already possess?

5. Can a teacher be effective without liking his or her subject?

5. Arthur W. Combs, *The Professional Education of Teachers* (Boston: Allyn and Bacon, 1965), pp. 44-45.

6. Many schools and teachers through educational practice tend to imply that the knowledge students remember is more important than the knowledge students look up. How would you evaluate this statement?

7. Describe the best teachers you have had the opportunity to work with in terms of scholarship as we have explored it in this chapter.

SELECTED REFERENCES

Archambault, Reginald D., ed. *Dewey on Education*. New York: Random House, 1966.

Chandler, B. J.; Powell, Daniel; and Hazard, William R. *Education and the New Teacher*. New York: Dodd, Mead, 1971.

Combs, Arthur W. *The Professional Education of Teachers*. Boston: Allyn and Bacon, 1965.

Glasser, William, M.D. *Schools without Failure*. New York: Harper and Row, 1969.

Haskew, Laurence D., and McLendon, Jonathon C. *This is Teaching*. Glenview, Illinois: Scott, Foresman, 1968.

Highet, Gilbert. *The Art of Teaching*. New York: Vintage Books, 1950.

James, William. *Talks to Teachers*. New York: W. W. Norton, 1958.

Joyce, Bruce, and Weil, Marsha. *Models of Teaching*. Englewood Cliffs, New Jersey: Prentice-Hall, 1972.

Ryan, Kevin, and Cooper, James M. *Those Who Can, Teach*. Boston: Houghton Mifflin, 1972.

124

THE
TEACHER:
A Decision Maker

Any decision made by a teacher is a reflection of his belief system.[1]

---

1. Dale L. Brubaker, *The Teacher as a Decision Maker* (Dubuque, Iowa: William C. Brown, 1970), p. 11.

Kimball Clark, a junior-high-school social-studies teacher in an urban area, has just had his late afternoon study session interrupted by Larry Wiles, one of his students. Larry, a student that Mr. Clark has been quite close to in class, has just entered his classroom and, standing before him, has thrown a quantity of pot on his desk. "I want to stop, Mr. Clark, but I just don't know how I'm going to. My mom and dad don't know about it. I didn't know who to go to...." What does Kimball Clark do now? What will his first reaction be? What should it be? How quickly must he react and what are his options?

In the midst of one of her parent-teacher conferences Eileen Cooper, a fifth-grade teacher, is confronted with this remark from a parent, "Last year Kathy was so tense most of the time because Miss Hass (a fourth-grade teacher next door) was constantly on her back for something or other. She even had her stay in from phys-ed class because she was caught talking one day when everyone was supposed to be completely silent when they waited in lunch line. Isn't that a bit strict for ten year olds? Do you believe that she was right to take her out of phys-ed class for that, just because she knew that it was one of Kathy's favorite classes?" What is Eileen Cooper's response to these questions? How does she handle this situation?

Mrs. Johnson has just been informed by her building principal that she will not be required to order textbooks for all her sixth-grade students in the area of science next year. He pointed out that she can spend the equivalent in other ways to support her science program. How should she use this money? What possibilities exist for her?

Glen Heathers, a first-year biology teacher in a suburban school district, has just examined a course of study that was given to him by the curriculum coordinator. He was told that it contained ten basic areas that were to be covered in his tenth-grade biology classes. Glen's reaction to the guide was quite negative. He disagreed quite strongly with some of the areas that were included in the guide and also some of the suggested approaches to the guide. What should he do about the situation? Should he supplement the guide with his own ideas without checking with anyone? Should he question or challenge the curriculum coordinator who seemed to feel strongly that all of the material should be covered? What decisions are called for in Glen's dilemma?

After examining the results of the standardized achievement tests that her fourth-grade class had recently taken, Mary Hamburg is about to take this and other information about her children and begin making follow-up instructional plans. With such a wide range of uniqueness represented in her group she is faced with many difficult concerns. What group possibilities exist for children with similar needs? What type of instructional materials will be best suited for each of these children? What instructional approaches would be most desirable? etc.

As a new teacher to the school district and the state, Morris Rondale had recently been approached by representatives of the two largest teacher organizations about his interest in membership. Although a large majority of the school district seemed to belong to the union-oriented group Morris was more impressed with the other organization. What should he do and what should be the important factors in his decision?

A math teacher at the senior-high level has just observed one of his students cheat in the middle of an important mathematics examination. Mary Tyler, the student, had quickly referred to a set of "crib notes"; to her knowledge no one in the class had seen her. What on-the-spot decision should the teacher make in this situation?

As a teacher, what kind of decisions would you make in each of the above episodes? Do you have enough information to make these decisions? If not, what additional information would be needed? What criteria would be applied to each of these decisions? Do you have a decision-making style? Are there different styles? Can you learn to make wiser decisions about the type of issues and situations that were reflected in these examples? What kind of decisions will you have to make as teacher? Let us begin with this question.

Teacher Decision Making: a Wide Arena

The teaching situations cited above are a limited sampling of the wide arena of responsibility for teacher decision making. Even though the examples share the limitation of not providing enough vital information for your critical response, they do point to several areas of concern for today's classroom teacher. *There are* schools where one could find detailed information about such problems, and *there are* classroom teachers who must make all of the decisions called for in the problems cited and, of course, in a multitude of other critical areas.

For example, teachers must make many decisions relating to people:

Who should be allowed to assist with instructional tasks?

How should they be used?

How should I approach Mary's parents who have a strong commitment to the A,B,C report cards?

How should I approach Mr. Johnson, the local postmaster, who talked over the heads of my fifth-grade class the last time he was invited in as a resource person?

Which of the parents should I choose to be homeroom parent hosts for the upcoming open house?

What approach should I use with Larry who appears to have a negative attitude about everything he does at school?

Should I have a private conference with Linda, who has been reported as a trouble-maker on the playground in the past few days?

Should I encourage David to try out for the debating team since I have noticed what I consider to be his potential in this area?

Teachers must also make a variety of decisions about instructional materials:

Which of the new instructional materials should I incorporate into my area of work and responsibility?

How should I go about the task of assessing which of these materials is most valuable?

How will I determine when it is most appropriate to show the film on death to my class?

Will the programmed materials on math be the most effective material for Betty at this time?

Should I incorporate the instructional television series, "Conservation: a Concern for All," into my ninth-grade conservation study?

Should each child have a copy of a basic text in my sixth-grade social-studies class?

How should I decide among a national curriculum project, a published program, and my own structured materials as a base for my social-studies program? Can I and should I use parts of all of them?

Organization is still another area around which numerous teacher decisions are called for. The following questions merely scratch the surface:

Should our school be graded or nongraded?

Which horizontal grouping pattern, team teaching, departmentalization, self-contained, etc., would best meet our needs? Should a combination of these organizational models be used?

When is homogeneous grouping a desirable organization option to be used and when is it inappropriate?

How can I decide, from among all the grouping options, which are most appropriate for the children in my class?

Should I divide my reading class into three groups for instructional purposes?

Should the school day be organized around major problem areas or themes, or around subject matter areas?

Decisions about content and instructional strategies are also called for by today's classroom teacher. The decisions are becoming more challenging and complex each year.

What will be the basic content goals for our school, my classroom, and more specifically, Johnny?

Should the study of history proceed from earlier historical events to present-day events or vice versa?

How will we decide what should be the major units of work in our science curriculum at the intermediate level?

On what basis shall I decide the appropriateness of inquiry-oriented teaching strategies, expository modes of instruction, etc.?

How will I decide when certain content dimensions of my program are outdated?

Under what circumstances will it be most desirable to utilize simulation and role-playing strategies with my class?

Should students play a more active role in determining appropriate content dimensions of their programs?

Should I decide to cover all areas prescribed in the course of study or take fewer areas and treat them in greater depth?

The area of curriculum development also creates many opportunities and situations that demand decision making on the part of classroom teachers. Even though this has been an area where the teacher has assumed a passive role in the past, changes in the last few years have moved today's teacher into a key decision-making position. Numerous complex decisions must be made.

What are the priorities for my school as far as curriculum study is concerned?

Who should be involved in our reevaluation of our social-studies program (teachers, administrators, students, lay individuals, college resource people)? What are their roles?

What criteria should be used in the self-study of the entire elementary education program in our district?

Should I volunteer to serve on the report card study committee even though it will mean a lot of additional work for me?

Should I agree to serve as chairman of ad hoc committee on school reorganization?

What curriculum development study organizations best meet our local needs (subject area committees, ad hoc problem-centered committees, grade-level study groups, total faculty approach, etc.)?

How can we utilize national and state curriculum study efforts and their findings in our curriculum development activity at the local level?

A number of decisions called for by a teacher are related to his or her professional role:

Which teacher organization should I belong to?

What professional associations do I want to become active in?

Should I pursue an advanced degree beyond the one I currently hold?

If so, which college or university would best meet my needs?

What decision should I make regarding my invitation to join the State Department Task Force to study and evaluate the quality of reading instruction at the state level?

Which of the fringe benefit proposals do I support in our staff negotiations for next year?

Should I arrange a conference with my supervisor to explore further the reasons why I was not promoted this past year?

Should I make a personal and professional decision to continue my writing and research activities even though time is not provided for such activity and it takes planning time away from my classes?

The list could be continued at some length with the addition of many other areas within which teacher decisions are called for: for example, time, money, classroom management, objectives, physical space. Some of these decisions will by necessity be on-the-spot decisions while others will provide the luxury of time and study. Some decisions will be natural to the teacher while others will be new and difficult to identify with. Some decisions will cause a great deal of anxiety while others will be made without even being aware they are being made. Some decisions will be made alone while others will be made in consultation with others. Some decisions will have positive results and some will be complete flops. The important thing, of course, is that *you* will be, or are involved in some way in all of these areas of decision making and the key question at this point is, *How will you make them?* Are there things that you can do to become a more effective decision maker? How will you behave in this world of decision making? What is your style? Are there different styles? How might I help you think through and sort out this element of your concept of teacher?

Some Modest Guidelines

If you are expecting that the following paragraphs will provide a foolproof model for effective decision making, it would perhaps be desirable for you to skip this section altogether. There have been a number of attempts to develop such models and, although they have added much to the quality of our understanding of this complex activity, they are by no means foolproof. The scientific method has been one of the most extensive of these efforts and even it lacks a quality of sophistication when applied to the complex world of classroom teaching. Therefore, the following are merely some modest guidelines that I personally feel are important to my concept of the teacher.

The first question I would ask is, What is your decision-making style? Do you know? How do you make decisions now, in or out of the classroom? Knowledge of your own personal style would appear to be an important prerequisite for any consideration for modification of style. This self-awareness can be brought about in a number of ways but perhaps the two most significant approaches are (1) ask people who know you personally and/ or work with you about your style and, of course, (2) the most obvious approach—ask yourself questions such as, Do I dislike making decisions? Do I rely on others to make decisions for me? Do I generally wait until the last minute to make decisions? Can I make quick, on-the-spot decisions with ease and confidence? Do I generally involve other people when I make decisions? Do I follow through on decisions I have made? Am I reluctant to make decisions that affect other people? Am I more uneasy about some decisions than others? If so, why is this the case? Am I generally thorough in considering all alternatives before making decisions? Do I make decisions on impulse?

Your answers to these and other related questions should provide you with major clues to your style, and it is this exposed style that I ask you to relate to the following guidelines. We all have our personal styles and the question is not so much how to take on a new style as it is to make the most of your present style in the educational setting, modifying it where necessary.

One of the first concerns in decision making is, Who should make the decision? There are many decisions, for example, that teachers make which should be made by students. Seating arrangements, landscaping the school grounds, certain portions of the schedule, and, yes, even certain aspects of what to teach and how to go about it might reasonably be a part of the student decision-making world. I believe we tend to make too many decisions for students and we might be well advised simply to stop more often and ask, Is this my decision to make?

The same concern exists for other people, such as administrators, parents, and supervisors. Perhaps parents should make more decisions about various aspects of the school and its operation. Maybe some decisions should involve a wider representation of your teaching colleagues than is present on a given committee on which you are serving. Maybe there are decisions, now being made by administrators and supervisors that should be made by the teaching staff. As obvious as it may seem, the question of who should make the decision is basic and as a new teacher or a veteran in the field any time spent on this portion of the decision-making process should reap rich dividends.

Another related dimension of decision making is when and how to utilize the input of others in making decisions. Even though you will ultimately be responsible for making a given decision, the judgments of others should frequently play an important role. Sometimes this judgment can be solicited from people directly; at other times it may be gleaned from writings. For example, a decision to have a child spend additional time in a unit, grade, or level should involve the combined judgments of a number of individuals, even though you as teacher are responsible in the final analysis. The parents, child, counselor, other involved teachers, etc., should have significant input into such a decision and it would seem to me a wise teacher who would solicit a variety of inputs from these individuals.

When you are called upon to make group decisions, such as a curriculum committee decision about an aspect of your program, the input of others can also be most helpful. For example, if the decision called for was to determine a major organizational framework for the school's social-studies program it would seem that the combined judgments of other teachers in the district, college resource personnel, professional writers in the field (through the literature), and perhaps the reactions of teachers and administrators from other school districts who were experimenting with a variety of models, would be most helpful. Inputs from these "significant others" would, in my estimation, add a degree of quality to the final decision that would be made by you and your teaching colleagues.

Do I have enough reliable information on which to base my decision? is another question in need of attention for teacher decision makers. When you are making a decision about a new program on a schoolwide level, or setting individual objectives for one child, it is important that you gather the most significant information related to the decision. As a beginning practitioner in the field you will bring to the classroom a rich knowledge and information background in terms of content, teaching strategies, knowledge of children and how they learn, and a variety of other areas. This information provides the base or foundation for many of the decisions you will have to make but, as any good experienced teacher knows, it is only a small part of the base upon which you build. You can't rely on that information alone to support the day-to-day classroom decisions that must be made. You will need to extend this information in many ways and add new sources of information based on the unique qualities of the district you work in and the specific students, parents, and teachers with whom you work.

For some decisions professional reading is involved, to gather the reliable information to back up a decision. Perhaps an examination of significant research findings would be in order. Maybe the information should be gathered through a person-to-person interview or discussion activity. If the decision involves a certain child in your classroom, perhaps it's a matter of simply visiting more with that child to gather the information that is germane. The question you will need to ask is, What kind of information do I need? The response to this question should suggest your approach and potential source. Test results (individual and group), information on new programs, parent attitudes, child feelings, information on new teaching strategies, cost factors, research statistics, etc., are only a small sampling of the different types of information that might be called for.

An example may be your need to make a decision about a fight that was reported to you on the playground involving one of your students. Because you didn't see the fight it would appear logical, before making any decisions, to hear out the person who reported the fight and anyone else who might have witnessed it. It is of course more important to gather information directly from the student who was supposedly involved.

Standing behind a decision (group or individual) and support-ing it is also significant in my concept of teacher. Even though you may not agree with all aspects of a group decision it would appear most desirable for you to support the decision, once made. This would not stand in the way of a continued professional effort on your part to work toward a change or modification in that decision. The decision-making process doesn't stop once the decision has been made. Support and follow-through are also vital ingre-dients, not to mention continued reevaluation of decisions made.

Being willing to honestly admit to poor decisions is another quality I feel strongly about in my concept of teacher decision making. We all make bad decisions from time to time and being comfortable in admitting that to colleagues, parents, and students can contribute richly to the respect you will have in your total decision-making framework. To be able to say, "Johnny, I really made the wrong decision to place you in this group, you should have been in group two," takes courage, a secure self-concept, and keen understanding of the importance of honest relationships between people. It would have been so easy to come up with "new information" of some sort to justify the change or, even more tragic, not to admit to the error and leave Johnny in the same group. Genuineness as we have explored it clearly relates to this dimension of a teacher's world as well.

To be fair in decision making, to know when to make decisions (on the spot vs. delaying), to have a rationale to support decisions, and to allow your decisions to be open for critical review are among other significant areas that relate to teacher decision making. Your ultimate goal of course will be to meet the needs of the learners with whom you work and your personal and professional needs as well. Your raw materials for decision making will be knowledge of yourself, knowledge of the learner, content, teaching strategies, and the many professional situations that you are or will be involved with. Your basic belief system will be your major guide. Go forth boldly.

Try Some on for Size

The following classroom and school episodes have been written by experienced teachers in the field. They represent real situations with which they have been confronted and for which teacher decisions were called for. How does your decision-making style apply to these situations? What decisions would you make? What additional information would you require before making any decisions? Who would you involve? Try some on for size.

Disagreement over Discipline

Whenever you send a student to the vice-principal for disciplinary reasons, the student returns with a note reprimanding you and the problem has not been treated. You lose control over these students who like to create trouble because nothing has been done to change their behavior. The students are friends of the vice-principal. Order and control start to break down. What do you do?

Pressure from Football Coach

You are planning to give a *D* to Jim Starr in your twelfth-grade class. The football coach approaches you and explains that a *D* on Jim's midsemester report will make him ineligible for the three remaining football games. As Jim is the star quarterback, this will almost surely cost the school the league championship. Further, the coach points out to you that Jim will do better after the league season is over and will have time to pull up his grade in your class. You doubt this as Jim's *D* is none too solid as it is but you also realize that playing football has been a primary factor in keeping Jim in school up to now.

What do you tell the coach?

Role Conflict: Policeman or Teacher?

Because of a recent water-balloon fight at the bus loading zone, you have been assigned to bus loading duty three weeks out of the school year. In addition to this you must also take your turn in supervising detention after school—a privilege which becomes yours about twice a month. Besides this you must also uphold many other specific rules around the school, such as hall passes for students in the hall during class time and many similar restrictions that all the teachers are required to enforce. You feel that the punitive image these responsibilities develop is highly detrimental to your relationship to the students. Your own philosophy is that an instructor should be a friend and a counselor as well as a teacher, and you really feel hampered by this situation.

What should you do?

A Lost Hat?

A first-grade child in my room lost her very nice, white furry winter hat. The next day another child from a poor family appears in school in an identical hat, which she said a neighbor gave to her.

What decisions do you make about the situation?

Your Reaction to the Romantic Involvement
of one of Your Students

You are a first-year male teacher, fresh out of college, and are teaching a freshman course. Over a period of weeks you notice that Betty has a crush on you and insists on lingering after class every day and running in to you as you leave school. The situation grows more serious, to the point of embarrassment. Betty constantly offers to help you collect papers, hand out assignments, and run general errands. You begin to sense resentment in the class for what appears to be your "favored" treatment of Betty.

What decisions are called for?

135

Lost Control?

The teacher from a room down the hall from mine one day knocked on my door and was in tears. She said she had lost control of her class and wanted me to go talk to her students.

What do I do?

Teacher-Teacher Relationship

A young teacher, who teaches in the same area that I do, has discipline problems with her junior-high class. All teachers and students with classes in that area can hear her "yell" at her class at the top of her voice. For instance, it is common for her to say, "Gentlemen, I am trying to conduct class so *shut up!*" For punishment, boys (numbering from 4-10) are put out in the hall and they start acting up and running around disrupting others in the area. She will come out in the hall and again yell at them. Because of class scheduling, I never see this person outside of class. By talking to other teachers who know her, it seems that she doesn't realize she is actually "yelling" at her class and creating problems in the area around her. As a teacher next to her, is it my responsibility to talk to her about this? If so, how do I go about it?

Teacher Sharing?

The teacher across the hall had gathered all the astronomy books from our library and refused to share. She had been studying astronomy for three weeks—I was beginning our astronomy unit.

What should I do?

In the Middle?

I found that I, as a new teacher, was being placed in the middle of personality conflicts between other teachers. Teachers with conflicts between themselves wanted me to take sides. It is a very uncomfortable position.

What should I do?

Administrator-Teacher Relations

One afternoon, after an unusually trying morning with my classes, my building principal stopped me in the main office and proceeded to reprimand me about an incident involving some of my students. The criticism of my handling of the original incident was deserved, but the office was full of teachers, students, and clerks.

What should my reaction be?

Student Pushes You and You Slap Him

Gene has been a problem child ever since he started school. He is now in your class and his behavior has not changed at all. You have tried in every way to reach him and nothing seems to be working. Finally one day you are at your wit's end; he is disturbing the class with his antics. You take him in the hall to talk to him and he becomes loud and outwardly rude. As you try to restrain him he pushes you and makes a motion as if to hit you. As a reflex, more than anything else, you slap him across the face.

What do you do?

Principal Asks You to Demonstrate Good Teaching for Fellow Teacher

You are a member of a secondary school's staff. You have taught in this school for two years and, therefore, do not have tenure. Another teacher, Mr. X, is new in the school and teaches the same subject and grade level you do. He has been having extreme difficulties in organizing his lessons. These difficulties do not seem to bother Mr. X, but the principal is very concerned. The principal calls you in and asks, "Would you consider taking over Mr. X's classes for a week while he observes you? I'll give you a couple of days to think it over."

What will your reaction be?

Teacher Organizations

During my first week in a suburban school, a fellow teacher came up to me and said, "If you want to get along in this school you had better join the X organization. All the good people are in this group and if you don't join this one, it will make you look bad. And besides, if you want to have any friends around this school, you have to be in this organization."

What decision should be made in this situation?

Teacher-Parent

After talking about the theory of evolution in class and treating it as a theory, one of the students brought a note from home saying in essence, "I would prefer that my son believe the definitive statements concerning creation of man in Genesis rather than the chance possibility of your evolution. He has been brought up in a Christian home and is a fine Christian boy. . . ."

Your Reaction?

What Did You Say?

At lavatory break time, my boys were not being as quiet as they should. I asked one boy to tell them to quiet down. This boy went in the lavatory, gave the rest my message, and I heard my problem child call me a "son of a bitch."

I decided to. . .

Teacher-Community

The teacher doesn't care to drink. He is invited by a citizen of the town to join him for a "short one" at the liquor store. Graciously declining the invitation he finds out that "anyone who won't have a beer with you" doesn't belong in the town.

Your reaction?

QUESTIONS FOR ANALYSIS

1. Should teachers assume more or less decision-making responsibility for what is taught in our schools? What are the reasons for your position?

2. What do you consider to be your major strengths in decision making? Your major weaknesses?

3. What decisions do you feel students should make in school?

4. From your viewpoint, what are some of the major decisions facing educators in the next decade? and beyond?

5. What role should parents play in educational decision making?

Brubaker, Dale L. *The Teacher as a Decision Maker.* Dubuque, Iowa: William C. Brown, 1970.

Doll, Ronald C. *Curriculum Improvement: Decision Making and Process.* Boston: Allyn and Bacon, 1965.

Haskew, Laurence D., and McLendon, Jonathon C. *This is Teaching.* Glenview, Illinois: Scott, Foresman, 1968.

Skeel, Dorothy J., and Hagen, Owen A. *The Process of Curriculum Change.* Pacific Palisades, Calif.: Goodyear Publishing Co., 1971.

NOTES

SECTION THREE

Potpourri

In setting out to explore the concept of the changing teacher, one thing was obvious—it would not be possible to cover adequately all of the important concerns and considerations that surround such a task. There are so many areas to be explored and space, time, and author limitations all have their bounds. Therefore, the purpose of Section Three is not to include all the areas of concern, but rather to provide an outlet for a few additional areas of concern which relate to my concept of teacher.

As a potpourri, then, I offer this section. Chapter 11, through a panel discussion among varied educators, poses many of the critical issues that surround the question: Is the teacher artist, clinician, or scientist? The inquiry mode of instruction and the role of the teacher is examined in Chapter 12.

Chapter 13 explores the legal world, the helper world, the professional world and a number of other worlds that surround the work of a teacher, while Chapter 14 analyzes teacher rewards.

Perhaps the most important chapter of all is Chapter 15—because you will write it.

140

THE
TEACHER:
Artist, Clinician, or Scientist?

*I believe that teaching is an art, not a science. It seems to me very
dangerous to apply the aims and methods of science to human beings
as individuals, although a statistical principle can often be used to
explain their behavior in large groups and a scientific diagnosis
of their physical structure is always valuable. But a "scientific" relationship between human beings is bound to be inadequate and
perhaps distorted. Of course it is necessary for anyone to be orderly
in planning his work and precise in his dealing with facts. But that
does not make his teaching "scientific." Teaching involves emotions,
which cannot be systematically appraised and employed, and
human values, which are quite outside the grasp of science. A
"scientifically" brought-up child would be a pitiable monster. A
"scientific" marriage would be only a thin and crippled version of a
true marriage. A "scientific" friendship would be as cold as a
chess problem. "Scientific" teaching, even of scientific subjects, will
be inadequate as long as both teachers and pupils are human
beings. Teaching is not like inducing a chemical reaction: it is much
more like painting a picture or making a piece of music, or on*

a lower level like planting a garden or writing a friendly letter. You must throw your heart into it, you must realize that it cannot all be done by formulas, or you will spoil your work, and your pupils, and yourself.[1]

142

The goal of any behavioral science, especially education and psychology, is to describe, account for, and predict human behavior. The knowledge obtained through the exercise of the science allows certain responsible professionals to control, change or order the behavior of other human beings and the world they live in. The behavioral scientist wants to know why certain individuals behave in the manner in which they do under certain specified conditions. He will also inquire into the results of planned intervention, testing to determine if such intervention at a given point

1. Gilbert Highet, *The Art of Teaching* (New York: Alfred A. Knopf, 1950), pp. vii-viii.

in time will produce more acceptable behavior. For example, the first grade teacher is a scientist. This professional has observed and hopefully recorded the behavior of human beings sufficiently to have identified certain patterns. Plans are constructed to intervene into the patterns that are brought into the classroom so that the human being exiting from this class will in many ways be a more socially acceptable person. At different levels of complexity, this is the most basic goal of education. Educators are interveners, changers, dissatisfied scientists—charged with the responsibility of manipulating human behavior. It is only in this context that the massive responsibility and power of the teacher becomes obvious.[2]

The teacher's role as artist, clinician, or scientist has been examined, analyzed and debated for many years. Even though firm conclusions are found only within individuals, the general ideas surrounding the debates help fill out many dimensions of a teacher's role.

Where do you stand as an individual in this debate? What are the implications for your role as teacher?

To assist you in sorting out your position and/or in questioning it, I have asked a representative group of students and educators with ranging interests and positions to address themselves to this issue; their spontaneous dialogue follows.[3] Collectively these individuals expose most of the critical issues revolving around the questions that started the discussion.

Are Teachers Artists, Clinicians, or Scientists?
Are They a Combination of These?

Boltuck: I think the teacher can be conceptualized as the scientist-technician, a model which I would like to push. It currently stems from the learning theory position. Within the classroom there are perhaps different types of activities on the teacher's part. One is the management of the students, types of things that unfortunately get in the category of discipline if they are

2. Joe L. Frost and G. Thomas Rowland, *Curricula for the Seventies* (Boston: Houghton Mifflin, 1969), pp. 71-72.

3. The members of the panel at St. Cloud State College are: Dr. Boyd Purdom, Professor of Elementary Education; Dr. Charles Boltuck, Professor of Psychology; Alice Patton, Elementary Education Major; Mary Phillips, Primary Unit Leader, Thomas Gray Campus Laboratory School; Phillip Tennison, Intermediate Unit Leader, Thomas Gray Campus Laboratory School; Dr. Roger Rouch, Professor of Elementary Education.

Also participating was Dr. Werner Tesmer, Principal, Birch Lake School, White Bear Lake, Minnesota.

not well managed. Another role of the teacher is the transmission of knowledge or training in the academic areas. Now take this role of the teacher as somebody who is responsible for training people and getting them to learn. Then the teacher can be conceptualized as a sort of reward machine, somebody that hopefully will be using positive rewards continuously or reinforcers. You can see some of this learning approach in the types of curriculum and equipment you see around the classroom today. The IPI approach, which is a series of sequenced tasks in small units (individually prescribed instruction). The influence of Skinner was originally focused on programmed instruction, followed rapidly by teaching machines, and more recently students are working on computer-assisted instruction and computer management instruction. I see this as the road the classroom teacher will be taking in the future.

Purdom: I feel the model of behavior modification infers too narrow a view of the learner. The learner is more than a machine reacting to his environment. Thus the teacher is more than pure scientist. The learner is a free active agent. The teacher's role is one of facilitating learning. The teacher consults and helps the learner build an evocative environment—one that suggests the choices and options that are available. The teacher's role is helping the learner get to wherever it is he wishes to go.

Patton: Dr. Boltuck, as a scientist, do you mean that the teacher would know what kinds of behavior she wants the child to do in advance? As a teacher, are you going to be able to say, "All right, by the end of this month, this week, this day, this child should be performing this way"?

Boltuck: Presumably, even if you want creative behaviors, conceptual behaviors, flexible types of behavior, these are not attained by chance. What I am suggesting is that the teacher's behavior is not whimsical, neither is the child's, but both are predictable behaviors under the control of certain variables. These can be precisely defined.

Tesmer: I don't think we have that much of a gulf between those two different opinions. I think most people agree that teachers should act as facilitators between the particular learning process. The idea that the teacher is the only source of learning in the classroom, I think, is going out. The imperial purveyor of education. So I think both sides would agree on the facilitator of learning. But looking at all the values which we have in education, the different structures which are possible, I can see various roles for teachers. I think there may be a point for many different points of view because we have seen that, as far as research indicates, many of the new innovations of education come up in comparative standings with no significant differences. Many of the things which we have been doing for several times. So it's sometimes awfully hard to convince the parents that one type of education is better than another, or one type of teaching is better than another. It seems to me that we want to put our emphasis on the word "learning" rather than the word "teaching." We learn from many different people. The teacher is one of the many resources available to provide learning for students. I think I would like to agree with you. I think you facilitate learning by being an artist sometimes and a scientist at other times.

Purdom: Many would say, that the part that is artist in me now, with just enough knowledge will become scientist later. I'm only artist in the sense that I am not sure how to explain exactly what it is that I'm doing. Fairly soon, once I'm able to identify that and put it into context, I can then use it to become scientific in approach. And I'm not so sure that I would want to agree with that position.

Rouch: In a sense I agree with Boyd that teachers are facilitators of learning but facilitators of learning in what respect? What learning? In that regard, it seems to me that the teacher also has to be a clinician in the sense of a person who can diagnose a particular skill, whatever it is you're working with. I mean diagnose in terms of a child's ability, and then go from that point on and facilitate learning. Now this implies more than just being able to diagnose; it also implies that they must know what they are diagnosing, the processes themselves. Now I don't see how you can have either by itself. In other words, you cannot have a strictly pure science and you also cannot have facilitative learning by itself because these are not separated.

Boltuck: Let me ask a question on what you mean by facilitator. Do you mean somebody that stands by and intervenes at strategic times?

Purdom: I'm not so sure I like the term "intervenes."

Boltuck: Well, I do. I guess that's why I used it. But "comes into motion and does things at certain times." That's what I mean by "intervenes"; "starts talking."

Tennison: You're probably suggesting more that you're available in case the child needs some kind of assistance in the learning process.

Purdom: I'm there to consult. I'm there to make some guesses about the kind of environmental setting that I can set up but also to allow the learner to suggest and manipulate the environment.

Rouch: But you do more than that?

Purdom: I'm not so sure.

Rouch: Again, I don't disagree that this is part of the role of the teacher, but it seems to me that there are some things that we want all people to be able to do. Specifically to be able to read, to be able to use arithmetic concepts, communicate with others, etc. I think that these are worthwhile goals for all people. Now I'm not so sure that all children by themselves will follow a path that will lead them to the completion of those goals. I think in a sense we do manipulate some of these people toward these ends.

Purdom: I am making an assumption, and I think the assumption has data to support it. All living organisms seek fulfillment. The person will seek fulfillment. And will actually do so in the absence of coercion. Now if I believe that, then as the teacher I can allow the student a great deal of freedom in making the kinds of decisions that significantly affect his life. If I don't, then I've got to manipulate, I've got to arrange the environment or the conditions so that he will learn that which is important for him to learn. But I would take the position that the learner is best able to decide that for himself and that I can provide him with a stimulating or evocative environment, one that might evoke something.

Boltuck: That's a more subtle form of manipulating. Providing a provocative environment if the environment is going to control the behavior. That's the stimulus control end of things. You're controlling the behavior through stimuli, I gather, rather than through the consequences of behavior.

Purdom: I made the statement when we first started that I would certainly agree that there are times when teaching is a science. You can't get away from that fact. But to allow the individual to come into that environment and make his choices, or to choose not to come into the environment, or choose to leave the environment is quite something else that I don't think you would allow as a teacher.

Boltuck: Not if I were trying to do something efficiently. I would allow it in the child that is self-generating. And by this I mean a child who has been on a particular schedule of rewards during his past so that he learns by himself. When I look at the college population here, and I'm sure it's a smaller population in the school system, I run into something like between 3 and 4 percent students who do that. That is, who have been so designed by their past experiences, if you want to call it that. I don't like the term. But by their past history of reinforcement which has been intermittent rather than continuous, so that now they function by themselves. They'll pick up a book, read, and learn from it. This is some 3 to 4 percent students. I'd be happy to leave those 3 or 4 percent alone to their own devices and not intercede, except maybe, I might want to make them aware of books, and bring some books to their attention, this kind of thing. And even then I would hope to program myself right off by giving them the skills on how to research and find materials on their own. So if they were going to learn calculus in their junior year in high school, this type of student is probably about that level; he should be able to know where to find a good calculus text and how to evaluate it on his own. I'd like to give him those skills. I'd like to have many more students do this, but the typical students that come to me, and I'm sure to you, are not people who learn on their own.

Tesmer: I'd like to come in here and say we are talking about the role of the teacher. Is there really one particular role which we can define? Don't we have many different roles? It seems to be a very beautiful theoretical discussion of what teachers ought to be as far as the total learning process is concerned, as far as child development is concerned, but isn't the role of the teacher in most cases delineated by what the ideas of the society are who are establishing this particular school? In other words, schools are suborganizations of society, and if society thinks about or has a particular perception of the role of the teacher and establishes these rules, then we bring individuals in to people those particular roles. And you may be the most artistically or scientifically oriented teacher, but regardless of what side you take *if it's somehow not congruent to what society thinks*, you aren't going to be successful in this world. You will either have to adapt or drop out.

Patton: Look at these two people [Purdom and Boltuck] in a school situation. In the same school they would have two different classes both functioning within the school. But they would make their own classroom an individual place. I mean obviously they have different ideas but they might both be able to survive, to be able to teach in the framework set upon them by their administrators and principals.

Rouch: There is something else that happens here too; it is not really what happens to me or Boyd or to anyone else, it is what happens to the children. Now perhaps a prior question we should ask is, What are the objectives we are setting out to accomplish? Now can we agree on these? Perhaps we did not start back far enough. What are the objectives of education, of elementary education in particular, since that is what most of us are involved with. Can we agree on this?

Boltuck: I think again on this question I am sure we will disagree on the way we initially phrase it. But I think we can probably each paraphrase it to other statements in such a way that we can get some agreement. The types of constructs that are being put forth by Boyd are completely foreign to myself in terms of the types of constructs that I am interested in coping with. On the other hand, I bet if he told me how he derived those constructs from what behavior he knows the child is self-propelling, then we could come to some type of agreement—possibly because again he must be inferring self-fulfillment in something.

Purdom: I would like to go back to a statement that was made not too long ago when you referred to efficiency. I think it is important in terms of what we are saying. I'm talking from a personal point of view. I'm not so sure that as a learner, I necessarily want to fulfill your expectations as my teacher of what you think is efficient for me. I want my own efficiency and I want to be able to determine what that is without it being imposed. When you say that an idea is OK but it's not very efficient, you're defining that in terms of what you consider efficiency to be, and I think from a scientific point of view I can understand that. But I'm saying that from a human point of view, I would like some say in that; I would also like to do things that aren't necessarily efficient.

Boltuck: I guess it's back to his statement, will society let you continue to function doing one math problem as a third-grade student to doing one math problem a year if that's what you decide. If society lets you function that way, fine. You may end up in a class with the mentally retarded and maybe society will let you function in that way. In that case, then society usually gives a role to the teacher in a class of the mentally retarded of trying to step that child up so he doesn't do just that one problem.

Purdom: That really doesn't have much faith in my ability to do those things in an efficient way for myself though, does it?

Boltuck: How do you get to the point where you have decided—I'll use your terminology—to do those things efficiently yourself? Is that not a consequence of what you've been through?

Purdom: I'm not so sure that it's a consequence of somebody's structuring at that point.

Boltuck: Well, I am. From everything I know from the lab, I am sure that people don't get to where they are whimsically. They get there as a result of some variables, and these can be specified.

Rouch: You know, we are a people of excesses. Regardless of what we do, we seem to go one way or the other in excess. Now I really can't see why we couldn't agree that there are things that we can give people decisions in, or children. But why can't we also agree that society dictates that there are things that you will do if you are going to be a successful and a productive member of that society? Now, if you accept the latter, then this means that in a school setting there are things that we must help people do. And one more thing, when you accept the philosophy that you are giving us, you are assuming that all children learn equally well. For example, I think it's very possible that some individuals have problems which hinder their ability to learn to read. Cause: not physical pain but mental anguish, let's say. I think it's also true that most people tend to stay away from those things which make them uncomfortable. If we let the person only do those things that he wants, we're going to have people going all the way through our system—we already have them as far as that goes, but that doesn't mean we shouldn't try and do something about it—but they will go all the way through the system, never learning these skills, communication skills, which will let them function effectively. I really think there needs to be room for both and I don't see how we can avoid it, but I don't think we can let people grow entirely in their own direction, or children, and say "You can do as you please, when you please and I will help you do it." I think there comes a time when we have to say, "I want to help you do this, I will help you do it, now how can I best do it?" And this is where the clinician comes in. Being able to diagnose, being able to tell where people are in terms of the development of a skill, then knowing what to do beyond that.

Phillips: I sort of wonder too about this role of the diagnostician in terms of efficiency. I think, if you think of efficiency as an end in itself, perhaps then you don't want to accept that term. But often times, you see a child breathe a sigh of relief when you have let him in on some way of getting over a hurdle that he has needed to get over. I really feel that, from this standpoint, your being able to know where he is and what his specific difficulty is and then just giving him a few techniques, is very important at some time in his life.

149

Tennison: The problem occurs before that, I think; the reason he felt that was such a hurdle to get over is because some kind of pressure was exerted on him, probably an extrinsic pressure of some kind, that he needed to do that, and I don't really think it's society's pressure. I think it's someone else's pressure who is mediating for society, "Kid, you need this and if you don't have it, you're going to be shook!" And so he gets shook, and then you give a little breath of fresh air, but another hurdle will come along. I think it's the kinds of pressures that we put on, the expectations that we build in, the timetables that we build in, to say that "Boy, if you're in the third grade and only working one problem a day then you're in trouble." It never occurred to the child, he's never run into society, real society that says you've got to work more than one problem a day. He's run into somebody who says, "Society is going to get you a barrel full of trouble."

Boltuck: Why be in trouble if you work one problem a day? Why not have nice things happen to you when you work five problems a day?

Tennison: Why not have nice things happen to you if you don't work any?

Boltuck: Because society won't let you function that way in the long run. So instead of that, why not set up this comfortable situation. I don't think that kids have to be uncomfortable in the classroom. I think the classroom should be a delightful place, where only rewards are meted out. And no punishments. I think you can shape up behaviors very beautifully that way.

Rouch: I'd like to respond to Phil for just a second. You mentioned hurdles, and I think we do place children in very uncomfortable positions because the hurdles we ask them to go over aren't much ahead of where they are. This is the fault of the teachers. I think teachers are accountable for what happens in a classroom, but I'm not so sure we're accountable for the achievement. This will come. We're accountable to know what to do. This is where accountability comes into the picture. This also implies again that you know, in reading, the process itself. If you know this you aren't going to ask a child to do something he can't do because if you understand the process you'll know where he is in terms of development and it goes on from that point. Too often we have —here's where the child is, here's where we are, and we expect him to bridge the gap. And this is the hurdle, he can't do it.

Tennison: I fully agree with that. I'd just like to help him when he says he needs help.

Rouch: Yes, but you've got to know what to do.

Tennison: Right! I'd love to fully understand the reading process.

Rouch: I'm just using reading as an example because I'm involved. You could use it with anything.

Tennison: The only thing that I'm disagreeing with is that I don't want to be the one to tell the child when it is he needs to hop that next hurdle. I think he's the one who needs to say that. He's the one who needs to make that decision.

Rouch: I don't think many children will really object to this, to moving on and progressing, if you structure it in such a way that they can.

Purdom: Who is it then who determines if I have the skill and the technology for manipulation of people? You know, it's nice to consider the fact that I'll use that kind of knowledge and manipulate for only good purposes. Then what do I do as an individual with a teacher who decides, I'll use it for other kinds. . . .

Boltuck: Ask a school principal what he will do when you misapply it. There are controls on your behavior. Ask our principal here.

Tesmer: We do have certain techniques now which enable us to assess the child as far as various skills in reading are concerned, and we have certain techniques which enable us to provide them with activities or experiences which will help them to move on. And then comes a time in which we have to give or be accountable in meeting with the parents, "What has this child achieved during this year?" And the question then comes up, Where have we come from? Where did he start and where did he go? We will have to find a way to explain to parents that this child made five giant leaps and this child didn't make any, which is very possible. We're going to even have to be accountable for that fact to say, Why did we not motivate this child? Why did we not get him interested in the task? Why did we not encourage him to do more than just sit there or go out and do something different? I cannot actually wait for the self-actualization because it seems to me that self-actualization is a process of success. If you are successful, you like to do more of this particular kind and that's where I think the responsibility of the teacher comes in regardless of whatever system you're using.

Rouch: Another point here. I believe that you said we do have diagnostic procedures becoming available, which we have not always had in the past. In fact this is rather a recent occurrence and as more of these are available, really diagnosis—not achievement, we're not talking about achievement in any sense. We're really talking about diagnosis, able to tell where individuals are in terms of development of skills, and then going from there. We are getting these, and I think if you look at the programs that are starting to emerge in various parts of the country, again using reading, you're going to see a diagnostic approach, prescription approach in this area of instruction. It's coming. You can see it developing. I don't see any other way. Certainly, what we've done has not been as successful as it might.

151

Purdom: Not only do I see that as an undesirable kind of thing but an impossible task. If I diagnose today, even if I'm capable of diagnosing 30 children exactly where they are in any given skill, let's say just one area, reading or whatever it is, as a result of my teaching hopefully something has happened to them. So what am I going to do? Come back and diagnose again tomorrow!

Rouch: In a sense you are, but in a sense you don't have to. What we're talking about here, again using reading, if we are aware of the skills that are learned in learning how to read, we can assess those that individuals know, or can find those that they don't know, and we can work with those that they don't know. This is what I mean by diagnostic teaching. Prescribing instruction based on this kind of diagnosis. Now, you could, as you have indicated, test every day. I don't think it's necessary, but you can go on beyond this. I wouldn't really have a great deal of faith in a doctor if I went into him and said, "Doc, I don't feel well," and he said, "You don't look well. Here, take ten or twelve pills. Maybe one of them will make you better." I would much rather he tried to find out what's wrong with me, prescribe medication for it. And hopefully, it's going to cure me, now it may not, but hopefully this is going to happen. And I think we can use this same approach in some of the areas in instruction, I'm not saying all. Here again, one of the problems, we either classify everything this way or nothing. I think areas such as math, reading, language arts, can be worked in this fashion.

Let me back up. If I could think of learning to read as going on a continuum, from going to a nonreader toward being an expert reader, however we want to define it. My job as a teacher is to move this individual as far along toward that point as I possibly can. Now to do this, I've got to be aware of the process itself. If I'm aware of that, then I can move him along. Now, granted there are many individuals that never go too far along this line, because of lack of ability, many factors, but still if I'm doing the job that I have to do, then I've got to be aware of that process, I've got to be aware of what to do with that individual to help him along. If we can look at it this way, then I guess we don't worry about grades; we don't worry about sick people; we don't worry about remedial programs. Because again it's really a matter of how far a person has moved. Regardless of how old he is. You can work with an adult, an illiterate, and use the same approach. Six or sixty, it makes no difference.

Tesmer: As far as I'm concerned, I still think that there is no one right way in order to educate children. I think what has been proved over and over again is that we have not been able to satisfy the various value structures which people hold. And anybody who feels they can satisfy all parents in their particular school, in their particular district, is quite an optimist. You know, the little boy who looks through all the horse manure in order to find his horse somewhere in there. I don't think that works. The ideas of alternatives of education that are being tried out in that south suburban school in Minneapolis are very good. I like to see that teachers have various ideas of what their particular job is as a teacher. I do feel there have to be differences here, so I think this discussion is healthy. It's very beautiful for people to make up their minds, because they may pick up one or two little ideas here and there. But I think in the long run they are going to adapt to the various situations in which they are going to be working. And they are going to look at the philosophy of education and they are going to look at what they've learned about their psychology of learning. And they are going to say, "These are my kids and how can I provide them with tasks which I know according to those two things—my education philosophy and my learning psychology—are good?" Regardless of that, you know I feel it would be nicer to be an artist than a clinician.

Boltuck: Can I just modify one of your statements slightly? I'm glad that the different positions are being presented as strongly as possible. But I think people shouldn't make up their minds, they should make up their behaviors.

Phillips: When you talk about rewards, Charlie, what are the kinds of rewards you see a teacher using in the classroom?

Boltuck: Teachers have forever used rewards, just like parents always do too. I've got a list of rewards that are two pages long at each age level. For the youngest kids, concrete rewards tend to be the ones that work best. For the next group of kids, social rewards, like praise, and things of this nature, you know, from junior high and high school. But the younger kids, more tangible rewards tend to be the ones that work. I can give you a long list of them. Teachers have been in first grade using stars and things on papers, or a mark on a paper, or a grade. These things have all been rewards in classrooms. Ultimately, social rewards would be the ones that take over, because these are the ones that will last outside of the classroom because that's what the kid brought us.

Tennison: You're really satisfied to condition him to only operate on the basis of reward?

Boltuck: That's what I guess Mary talks about when they talk about love, positive reinforcement. I think this is a very good basis for behavior. Now what I would like to do is to get the child so that he needs very very little of this. The way you do that is by gradually thinning down the amount of reward you use.

Tennison: Would you not also believe the answer to this question is, Yes, rewards are better than punishments.

Boltuck: That I think I said before.

Phillips: I just heard two concrete examples that come to mind. I visited the Montessori school this fall, and the teacher there says she never gives any child a reward or any kind of praise unless he comes to her with it to show it to her, in a sense asking for it.

Boltuck: If she does that once, she's got him coming to her more frequently. But the second thing is that discovery methods work strictly on a reward principle. You know, you finish a jigsaw puzzle, that's pretty reinforcing. So if you discover how numbers work or how to put a puzzle together, you've had natural reinforcers built into those things. Discovery method is reinforcing but it's a slow method, I mean it's not the best, because you can't hand out rewards as frequently as you would want to. To learn how to do third-grade arithmetic you have to hand out 30,000 reinforcers or something.

Phillips: I also heard a teacher in the British primary schools make a statement that she doesn't comment on a child's picture, that art is very strong in schools because the next picture the child makes will be to please her, rather than to please himself.

Boltuck: The child has self-control procedures that are already built into him by prior things. In other words, people have reinforced him enough in making pictures and things like this in the past. And you would want to reinforce, obviously, an artistic kid. Have you ever seen a kid make a drawing and bring it to a parent, where the parent doesn't fawn on the kid?

Phillips: Yes, I have.

Boltuck: What happens to those kids?

Phillips: They don't want to perform.

Purdom: Is there a difference, using the illustration of the picture, between the teacher saying "That's a nice picture," and approaching the child on the basis of "How do you feel about your picture?" and the child says "I like my picture," and you comment "I'm glad that you like your picture."

Boltuck: If that's what turns him on. If that's what gets responses.

Purdom: No. I don't see that you've rewarded the picture or the drawing of the picture.

Boltuck: What I would like to do, of course, is to train the kid to make pictures on his own without having to come to me for rewards. Frankly, I'm not interested in how the other child feels because I don't know how to get a fact; all I can get are verbal statements, very often which contradict other statements which look like what you and I have learned to assess as his feelings. So verbal statements are not a good criteria for whatever your common feelings say, any more than the person saying, "I'm going to vote this way in the voting booth," is a direct statement that he's going to vote that way. So I guess I'm not that interested in dealing with that kind of behavior. Now I know a lot of the educational sphere is talked up about the emotional realm and all this kind of thing. I would rather see what are the behaviors that teachers are talking about when they are talking about the emotional realm, and let's deal with those. Now I am sure that when you tell kids they've made a good painting or say, "Hey, come over here and look at this painting," or bring the other teachers and the kids, or send it to the office to let the principal see it, etc., and he pats the kid on the back—where you have a whole reinforcing environment around the kid, the kid is going to tell you, "Gee, I like that picture."

And on the discussion goes—pros, cons, attempts at mediating positions, and the continued unearthing of issues relating to the teacher's role as scientist, clinician, or artist. *Where do you stand?*

1. How would you analyze the two opening quotes by Highet and Frost and Rowland? What do you consider to be the strengths and weaknesses in their points of view?

2. Which do you think were the strongest arguments presented in the dialogue of the panel of educators shared in this chapter? What would you have added if you had been a member of the panel?

3. How would you respond to an individual who said, "We are living in a scientific day and age and teachers need to operate from a scientific base in their work with children"?

4. What would you say to an individual who told you that teachers are born, not made?

155

5. What do you consider to be the major strengths and weaknesses of the clinician concept of the teacher?

6. Try to recall a few of your favorite teachers and try to describe them in terms of the categories of artist, clinician, and/or scientist? Is there a pattern?

SELECTED REFERENCES

Abraham, Willard. *Time for Teaching*. New York: Harper and Row, Publishers, 1964.

Ashton-Warner, Sylvia. *Teacher*. New York: Simon and Schuster, 1963.

Bruner, Jerome S. *The Process of Education*. New York: Vintage Books, 1960.

Coleman, John E. *The Master Teachers and the Art of Teaching*. New York: Pitman, 1967.

Frost, Joe L., and Rowland, G. Thomas. *Curricula for the Seventies: Early Childhood Through Early Adolescence*. Boston: Houghton Mifflin, 1969.

Hass, Glen; Wiles, Kimball; Cooper, Joyce; Michalak, Dan, eds. *Readings in Elementary Teaching*. Boston: Allyn and Bacon, 1971.

Highet, Gilbert. *The Art of Teaching*. New York: Vintage Books, 1950.

Holt, John. *How Children Learn*. New York: Pitman, 1969.

Hyman, Ronald T. *Teaching: Vantage Points for Study*. Philadelphia: J. B. Lippincott, 1968.

James, William. *Talks to Teachers.* New York: W. W. Norton, 1958.

Joyce, Bruce, and Weil, Marsha. *Models of Teaching.* Englewood Cliffs, New Jersey: Prentice-Hall, 1972.

Ohles, John F. *Introduction to Teaching.* New York: Random House, 1970.

Skinner, B. F. "The Science of Learning and the Art of Teaching." *Harvard Educational Review* 24 (Spring, 1954): 86-97.

———. *The Technology of Teaching.* New York: Appleton-Century-Crofts, 1968.

NOTES

THE
TEACHER:
Why Inquiry?

*No matter how well subject matter is presented, it will have no
effect upon the student until he has become personally involved in the
learning process. Learning is not passive. It is an active process,
requiring a personal commitment on the part of the learner.*[1]

1. Arthur W. Combs, *The Professional Education of Teachers* (Boston:
Allyn and Bacon, 1965), p. 49.

Indeed, learning is not passive and the role of the teacher, as we have suggested in earlier portions of this analysis, is to activate the learner, and help him to grow and develop through his own power and motivation. One of the most significant tools the teacher has at his or her disposal is the inquiry-oriented teaching strategy which places the student in the central role in the educative process. In this approach to classroom instruction the student must be active, not passive.

To add this dimension to my concept of teacher, I should like at this point to share an article which focuses on the why of inquiring strategies as well as on the role of student and teacher.

"Why Inquiry?"[2]

Of all the questions that can be asked about investigation-oriented teaching methods, whether they are called inquiry, problem solving, reflective thinking, or discovery, the most fundamental one is "Why?" This deceptively simple question has concerned educators for many years, and numerous individuals[3] in their own styles and from their own vantage points have advocated such investigation-oriented approaches through their writings and have pressed for refinement of responses to the question "Why inquiry?" The focus of this analysis is also centered on this fundamental question, and although the temptation is great to frame a case for inquiry around the respected and eloquent words of recognized authorities, the authors have chosen to use words of the less-heard-from authorities—children. Before calling for their assistance, a few words of introduction are needed to clarify the general dimensions of the inquiry approach.

Although it is impossible to offer here a set of refined and adequately researched dimensions of inquiry approaches agreed on by all educators, it is becoming increasingly clear that for many of our educational purposes such approaches are superior to the expository mode of classroom instruction. These approaches seem to share the common goal of having the pupil assume the central role in the educative process and become an active inquirer in his own education as opposed to the passive role of the learner,

158

2. Owen A. Hagen and Steve T. Stansberry, "Why Inquiry?" *Social Education* 33, no. 5 (May 1969): 534-537.

3. Ernest E. Bayles, *Theory and Practice of Teaching* (New York:Harper and Row, Publishers 1950); Jerome S. Bruner, *On Knowing: Essays for the Left Hand* (Cambridge: Harvard University Press, 1962); John Dewey, *Logic: The Theory of Inquiry* (New York: Holt, 1938); Jean Fair and Fannie R. Shaftel, eds., "Effective Thinking in the Social Studies," *Thirty-seventh Yearbook of the National Council for the Social Studies* (Washington, D.C., 1967); Bernice Goldmark, *Social Studies: A Method of Inquiry* (Belmont, California: Wadsworth, 1968); Gordon H. Hullfish and Philip A. Smith, *Reflective Thinking: The Method of Education* (New York: Dodd, Mead, 1961); Byron Massialas and Benjamin Cox, *Inquiry in Social Studies* (New York: McGraw-Hill, 1966).

which is often, but not always, characteristic of expository teaching. In the latter the pupil generally assumes the role of the respondent to questions posed by the classroom teacher and rarely raises questions himself. He tends to spend most of his time listening to what the teacher has to say about a topic rather than engaging in classroom dialogue with his peers and with the teacher. In short, he is teacher dependent. Inquiry strategies more frequently engage the pupil in decision making regarding his own instruction. The pupil in this approach assumes an active role in activities relating to his own learning and generally interacts with his peers and his teacher to a larger degree. The inquiry approach is a student-centered mode of instruction rather than teacher-centered.

John Dewey[4] made one of the earliest and most significant protests against a curriculum based on the teaching of specific facts and generalizations. He maintained that true education is not only the transmission of accumulated knowledge but also a process of assisting the development of certain natural tendencies of the child. One such tendency is to inquire: i.e. wanting and trying to find out. He also believed that such inquiry, together with learning how to search effectively for answers to questions raised, is more important than learning particular information. The development of such inquiry and procedures for seeking answers is useful to the pupil in any situation that might confront him. Dewey viewed facts as meanings that have already been established and that should be used as resources for conducting new inquiries, which lead to new information, concepts, and generalizations.

Although there are numerous contemporary vantage points from which to view the inquiry approach, Carpenter provides a firm operating foundation when she suggests that: "Inquiry is considered to be the process by which a child, more or less independently, comes to perceive relationships among factors in his environment or between ideas that previously had no meaningful connection."[5] She sees new understandings evolving through application and reorganization of past experiences on the part of the pupils and further relates that insights and self-confidence grow as the child successfully meets situations of increasing abstractness and complexity, i.e., as he moves up the ladder from observation, classification, and application to generalization. Perhaps the following well-chosen words best reflect the "pulse" of the inquiry approach:

Thus the inquiry approach views the learner as an active thinker—seeking, probing, processing data from his environment toward a variety of destinations along paths best suited to his own mental characteristics. It rejects passiveness as an ingredient of effective learning and the concept of the mind as a reservoir for the storage of knowledge presented through

4. John Dewey, *Democracy and Education* (New York: Macmillan, 1916).
5. Helen McCracken Carpenter, "The Role of Skills in Elementary Social Studies," *Social Education* 31 (March 1967): 219-221.

expository instruction directed toward a predetermined, closed end. The inquiry method seeks to avoid the dangers of rote memorization and verbalization as well as the hazard of fostering dependency in citizens as learners and thinkers. . . . The measure of ultimate success in education through inquiry lies in the degree to which the teacher becomes unnecessary as a guide.[6]

In short, the pupil assumes the central role, or at least works from a more cooperative position with the teacher than is generally the case in the expository mode of classroom instruction. He becomes more of a questioner himself and less of a respondent to the questions of the teacher, facilitating to a larger degree self-discovery of certain basic concepts and principles.

Despite the strong philosophical case for the inquiry approach, one is somewhat alarmed by what appears to be a very strong verbal commitment without much evidence of inquiry approaches in actual practice. In short, we do not seem to be practicing what we believe to the extent that would be desirable in our classrooms.

Even though we are experiencing this instructional lag, there is still the need for continued discussion of the value and desirability of inquiry approaches in the literature. As previously noted, various champions of inquiry seem to have followed through with this responsibility. There is, however, one sound to these recurring messages that is noticeably absent. This is the sound of children, and it is this "new sound" that we draw upon in offering a case for the inquiry approach.

The "new sound of children" incorporated within the following discussion is taken from actual statements of pupils. These personal perceptions were solicited by the authors in interviews with a single group of 30 sixth-grade pupils engaged in an inquiry-oriented unit of study reflecting much of the spirit of the inquiry approach and philosophy expressed by Carpenter. No claim is made for having solicited the true perceptions of children, and the responses have been treated only as "reported perceptions." No claim is made that these reported perceptions are reflective of all children everywhere. On the contrary we are simply using the language of a handful of pupils to assist us in communicating to the reader elements of a strong case for the inquiry approach.

In building or restating such a case one is immediately drawn to the possibilities within the inquiry process for developing a more responsible, self-directed, and active pupil in the learning process. Indeed, the literature abounds with statements that frame the importance of developing pupil characteristics leading to active involvement as well as statements that encourage and endorse inquiry. Children also sense the value of active involvement, and, although the words they have available to express their feelings might not be the same as those found in the literature, this in no way detracts from the

6. Ibid., p. 220.

importance of the message they have to share. For example, one sixth-grade girl in commenting on her experiences in an inquiry-based unit of study states: "It gets kinda boring to just sit and listen to someone who is always talking. It's kinda fun to make decisions for yourself and think about it instead of having someone tell you all the time." Another girl after having made essentially the same statement adds an important reason for her position when she relates: "It would help a lot if they (teachers) just wouldn't talk so much and give us something to do, because more gets through to you if you are working yourself and making decisions."

One boy, in sharing feelings about his involvement in the inquiry-based unit, seems to touch at the very quick of the development of pupil independence when he says: "We have to be able to be independent. We can't always be asking the teacher what everything is—like I have developed a way of just trying not to ask the teacher everything. But sometimes that's hard too, so you have to ask some things." Once again, although the words at times may tumble over one another, the message is clear.

The inquiry process would also appear to contribute to a posi- **161** tive desire to learn on the part of the pupil. This is because primarily the inquiry process facilitates and encourages a personal identification with areas of study within the school program. It is an ego-directed process by which the individual "consciously defines his problem and his terms, marshals his data, tests and verifies his hunches, judges the evidence, and systematizes the knowledge he has obtained."[7] Indeed, he is dealing with problems from his frame of reference, and in so doing it would seem that he is not just conducting an indiscriminate search for facts. On the contrary he is pursuing meanings and understandings that are real and important to him and at the same time making decisions about their significance. This personal involvement would appear to be a prerequisite for stimulated inquiry into any field of knowledge because what the material will mean to the pupil cannot be predetermined by the instructor. All he can do is to create, to the best of his ability, a working environment conducive to stimulating inquiry. Because motivation is essentially a personal matter, whether a pupil is motivated to learn can only be determined by the pupil himself.

The teacher who in one way or another *compels* students to learn certain things at a particular time and in a particular way, complicates an already confused situation, viz., the struggle of the student to find himself. He unwittingly projects his own will-struggle into the learning-teaching activity, not skillfully and professionally, but as one who, personally, has something at stake. This robs the student of the chance to discover himself.[8]

7. Charlotte Crabtree, "Supporting Reflective Thinking in the Classroom," Effective Thinking in the Social Studies, *Thirty-seventh Yearbook of the National Council for the Social Studies* (Washington, D.C., 1967), p. 87.

8. Nathaniel Cantor, *The Dynamics of Learning* (Buffalo: Foster and Stewart, 1950), p. 275.

It would be somewhat of an oversimplification to state that we cannot afford to allow these "robberies" to occur. Take it from the pupil who says: "I think you learn more than the book gives you. You work in the book and, well, you mostly just forget it. If you do it yourself, you are more interested and you remember it longer." Or another pupil commented: "It's kinda like you're really important because you're planning everything—you're really doing it." Sometimes the reasons were not always clear to the pupil, but again the message comes through: "I really don't know why—it just makes you want to do it more. The books aren't as fun when you just copy down a couple of sentences and answer the questions and stuff."

The key to how successful we will be in providing for this high level of motivation lies in the extent to which intrinsic rather than continually directed extrinsic rewards guide the thoughts and actions of pupils. Learning is personal and only takes place within the learner; therefore, teachers, at best, serve as mediators with the basic task of creating situations where pupils are brought into meaningful confrontation with important areas of concern within the social-studies program. Do pupils view the teacher's role in this way? We will let you be the judge: "There is teaching where the teacher tells you what to do, and one where the teacher just talks and talks, and then there's the kind where we help decide what to do. That's what we are doing in social studies, and it's really fun."

A further advantage of the inquiry approach is that it should contribute to "learning how to learn," or what Bruner refers to as learning the heuristics of discovery.[9] What do the pupils say? "We get a lot of new ideas from working in groups. I learn more than reading a book. When I read a book, I can be thinking about something else—here I have to be thinking about it all the time." Another pupil puts it this way: "Well, I like it because we can do it ourselves, and you don't always have to have the teacher looking right over you to make sure you're doing it. You just feel more relaxed about it, and everything, and you are learning how to find answers to questions." In short, as one sixth-grade philosopher so eloquently expresses it: "You couldn't learn anything if the teacher told you everything." The authors would agree and add that you can't learn how to learn unless you are given practice in inquiry and the opportunity to figure out things for yourself. As Bruner states it: "Of only one thing am I convinced: I have never seen anybody improve in the art and technique of inquiry by any means other than engaging in inquiry."[10]

The possibility that the process of inquiry effectively facilitates important thinking operations such as comparing, summarizing, observing, interpreting, and criticizing is also discussed at length in the literature. Although the reported perceptions of children understandably do not reflect

162

9. Jerome S. Bruner, *On Knowing: Essays for the Left Hand* (Cambridge: Harvard University Press, 1962), p. 92.

10. Ibid., p. 94.

in great detail on these thinking operations, there were numerous reactions that appeared on the fringe of what they had to say about other matters. For example, one boy, in commenting on the dynamics of group discussion and debate, related that: "We can give our own ideas and if someone thinks up an idea we don't always have to go along with it—we can do it another way." It would seem that such freedom to openly debate and critically analyze issues contributes to the refinement of important thinking operations. The beauty of reaching certain destinations in harmony after a period of group debate and refinement comes through in one girl's deceptively simple statement when she relates: "Yes, we have a lot of disagreements—like sometimes we make suggestions when we discuss something and sometimes we have little arguments, but we turn out all right."

The inquiry approach does not guarantee, however, that such debate and analysis of issues is automatically inherent in the learning process. The following statement offered by a girl might serve as a caution in this respect: "The other girl in my group made all of the decisions, and all I did was write them down."

163

The importance of recognizing and comparing various viewpoints as an important thinking operation comes alive in the following remark regarding references: "You need to be able to look for lots of references and find out what they say. You can't just look at one book and say that's what it is, because I have seen lots of books that have different stories but are based on the same thing." Such opportunities that relate to a variety of thinking operations would appear to be more easily facilitated and realized through inquiry than through an expository approach to classroom instruction.

An additional advantage realized through the inquiry process is that this approach should provide a natural springboard for the transfer of learning. Indeed, if learning is to broaden the individual's potential for effective behavior in and out of school, the learner must see the relation of the current learning to his life and must be able to recognize situations where the new understanding or skill is appropriate and apply it.

The pupils interviewed had very limited experience with inquiry procedures. Perhaps even more limiting was the lack of ability of the interviewers to ask truly appropriate questions of these children to determine meaningful transfer. A few comments made by the children seemed to indicate, however, that they were indeed transferring learnings from subjects and previous experiences to solve their immediate problems. As one boy stated: "You can really tell who has learned from last year. You know who has really gotten something out of what you have studied before. He is the guy that can correct things and know what to do."

Another pupil remarked about his experience in creating new laws for an imaginary state the class was developing: "It's not easy to make up laws. You've got to find a certain one that everybody likes. If nobody likes it, like if one man like a dictator makes up a law—say he made up a law nobody liked—they wouldn't follow it." Here we see an attempt to express a point that the pupil has not clearly thought out, but certainly there is an attempt to relate previous learnings to a problem at hand.

There are, undoubtedly, numerous other potential advantages of investigation-oriented approaches such as their contribution to greater self-confidence on the part of the pupils, greater retention, and a more positive attitude toward social studies in general. To be all inclusive, however, was never our purpose in this analysis, and although the sounds of children could go on, perhaps the setting should change from this article to your classroom. The sounds are there if we would listen.

In conclusion it might be well to reiterate that it has not been our purpose in this article to create a new case for the process of inquiry, rather it has been to restate with a new sound the strong case that already exists. Continued experimentation and refinement are called for as many questions remain unanswered and are in need of attention. Among them: Are all pupils suited for the inquiry approach? Do some pupils learn more effectively via another approach? Does the inquiry process accommodate all learning styles? How much of the program should be devoted to inquiry? Is there a danger of the inquiry process becoming a ritual? These are only a sampling of issues that demand our attention as we press for refinement of inquiry strategies. It is a challenging and difficult task, but then as one pupil so aptly expressed it: "Sure it's a little harder—but it's funner too!"

QUESTIONS FOR ANALYSIS

1. How could you be instrumental in your school or classroom in assisting learners to assume a more active role in the learning process?

2. In what ways have teachers "robbed" children of opportunities to discover themselves through the process of inquiry? How can this be avoided in the future?

3. In what situations would inquiry-oriented strategies appear to be more desirable than the expository mode of instruction? In what situations might the reverse be true?

4. How would you respond to a parent who said, "I don't believe in the idea that children should spend all that time trying to find out answers the teacher already knows. It's the teacher's job to tell the kids. That's what we pay them for."

5. In what ways do you think the process of inquiry facilitates important thinking operations such as comparing, summarizing, interpreting, etc.?

6. Does the inquiry approach fit your personal teaching style? Why or why not?

SELECTED REFERENCES

Bayles, Ernest E. *Theory and Practice of Teaching.* New York: Harper and Row, 1950.

Bruner, Jerome S. *On Knowing: Essays for the Left Hand.* Cambridge: Harvard University Press, 1962.

Cantor, Nathaniel. *The Dynamics of Learning.* Buffalo: Foster and Stewart, 1950.

Carpenter, Helen McCracken. "The Role of Skills in Elementary Social Studies." *Social Education* 31 (March 1967): 219-221.

Combs, Arthur W. *The Professional Education of Teachers.* Boston: Allyn and Bacon, 1965.

Crabtree, Charlotte. "Supporting Reflective Thinking in the Classroom." In *Thirty-seventh Yearbook of the National Council for the Social Studies.* Washington, D.C., 1967.

Dewey, John. *Democracy and Education.* New York: Macmillan, 1916.

———. *Logic: The Theory of Inquiry.* New York: Holt, Rinehart and Winston, 1938.

Fair, Jean, and Shaftel, Fannie R., eds. "Effective Thinking in the Social Studies." In *Thirty-seventh Yearbook of the National Council for the Social Studies.* Washington, D.C., 1967.

Goldmark, Bernice. *Social Studies: A Method of Inquiry.* Belmont, California: Wadsworth, 1968.

Hagen, Owen A., and Stansberry, Steven T. "Why Inquiry?" *Social Education* 33 (May 1969): 534-537.

Hullfish, Gordon H., and Smith, Phillip A. *Reflective Thinking: The Method of Education.* New York: Dodd, Mead, 1961.

Massialas, Byron, and Cox, Benjamin. *Inquiry in Social Studies.* New York: McGraw-Hill, 1966.

166

THE
TEACHER:
Many Worlds

Today's teachers are expected to. . .

1. *Remain alert to significant developments in academic specialty and continue general education in order to avoid obsolescence of knowledge.*

2. *Be a continuing student of the educative process and keep current with respect to innovations in teaching methods and materials.*

3. *Plan with students and fellow teachers.*

4. *Work with curriculum committees.*

5. *Experiment with different content, methods, and materials and keep systematic records of such studies.*

6. *Read and evaluate student work.*

7. *Confer with students and parents regarding pupil progress.*

8. *Counsel and advise students on academic, vocational, and personal concerns.*

9. Maintain a cumulative file of significant data on each student.

10. Develop reading lists, outlines, study guides, drill sheets, and visual materials.

11. Prepare tests appropriate to the range of objectives established.

12. Type and duplicate tests and other materials for classroom use.

13. Arrange for field trips, outside speakers, and other programs relevant to the learning objectives of the class.

14. Supervise homeroom, study hall, or lunchroom.

15. Supervise playground or recess periods.

16. Advise student extracurricular groups, chaperon school functions.

17. Keep attendance and academic records.

18. Collect money for various drives and sell tickets for school events.

19. Order and return films and other visual aids and operate equipment involved.

20. Participate in professional-association and learned-society activities.

21. Maintain an active interest in civic and community affairs and represent the school in the community effectively.

22. Orient and assist beginning teachers.

23. Supervise student teachers and cooperate with area colleges in providing opportunities for observation and demonstration.[1]

1. George W. Denemark, "The Teacher and His Staff," *N.E.A. Journal* (December 1966), p. 4.

To be a teacher is to live in many worlds. As you can see from the incomplete list of expectations above, these worlds touch many areas. Although they all overlap to a certain extent the unique aspects of these many worlds makes the task of today's teacher very complex. We have already explored many of these worlds in previous portions of this analysis so the purpose of this chapter will be to briefly probe a few additional "worlds" to help round out dimensions of my concept of teacher. Let us begin with one of the most rapidly growing worlds of all—the world of technology.

The World of Technology

The world of technology surrounds today's teacher in many ways. There is, for example, the general massive impact of technology on the lives of the students he or she works with. Consider the following very brief set of examples and ask yourself, What impact do these developments have in the world of education?

Elaborate transportation systems which link nearly all parts of our world

Television (not only in the home, but in several rooms of the home)

1,000 books per day being published in the world

Man travels to the moon and back

Thousands of acres of land being covered with concrete or blacktopping each week

Domed all-weather stations (and even cities) being planned and developed

Heart and other vital human organ transplants along with major medical advancements which continue to stretch man's life expectancy

Computers doing work in minutes that would have taxed hundreds of men for days, weeks, and even years

Power being tapped in new ways to serve man—electric toothbrushes, garbage disposals, blankets, knives, mowers, garage door openers, window openers, and you name it.

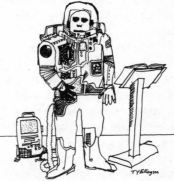

There can be little or no doubt that technology developments do influence the teacher's working relationship with students. In a society such as ours the goal of providing an individual with a set of skills that will carry him through life is a thing of the past. We have seen for example new fields rise, flourish, and become outdated within a time span of 15 years. We have seen the computer make some jobs obsolete. Such rapidly changing knowledge gives the teacher and the schools perhaps the largest and most important educational challenge of all: to provide students with self-learning skills and abilities, and motivation for their application after-formal schooling has ended. This of course is not a new thought but the importance of it appears to have increased.

The teacher is also faced with the challenge of working with an increased and even more complex set of uniquenesses in children based on their experiences with the technological world about them. For example, it does appear to make a difference in the teacher's approach when in his class are children who: (1) have traveled extensively vs. those who haven't; (2) have access to power in terms of snowmobiles, hondas, cars, televisions, stereo equipment, etc., vs. those who do not; (3) have access to all types of literature vs. those who do not; (4) have homes with all the benefits of modern technology vs. those who do not, and on the list goes. My intention in mentioning these examples is not to place them in good-bad or right-wrong categories but simply to emphasize that the teacher, in order to be successful, must understand each child's physical frame of reference, and a rapidly changing world of technology is making this task even more challenging than it has been in the past.

Teachers must also be able to utilize technology in effective ways in the teaching process. Here again the world of technology has expanded greatly in the past few years. Teaching machines of many shapes, forms, and purposes have been and are being developed: computer-based instruction is growing rapidly; instructional and educational television continues to have a significant impact in many areas; programmed learning devices are readily available to teachers at all levels; scientific equipment of all sorts is being developed for teacher and student use; cassette recorders and projectors of a variety of sorts are designed in such a way that they can be used by students at home as well as in the classroom; reproduced artifacts are available, and the list goes on.

All of this instructional hardware and much more is available to today's classroom teacher. What is the teacher's role in the utilization of these materials? Do such developments have a significant effect on the relationships of students and teachers? Who should design the software that will be used in teaching machines and other instructional devices? What about the cost factor? How will you as teacher keep all of these developments in proper perspective as you go about your day-to-day work with children? One thing is certain, schools and teachers cannot escape the influence of a rapidly changing technology. As Peter Drucker so clearly expresses it:

Like most other elements of contemporary life, education can scarcely escape the influence of continuing technological developments that rapidly change some ways of living. Indeed, as seen by the author of this selection, technology promises in several respects to foster and expand the role of formal education. But further advancements in technology and expanded schooling portend an increased variety of educational responsibilities. These include the necessity for schooling to change considerably more rapidly than it has in the past. Can schools meet the challenge?[2]

The Helper World

Another world that surrounds the work of a teacher is the helper world (teacher aides, resource personnel, lay participators, etc.) which appears to be a rapidly enlarging world. Teachers have had individuals assist with the work of the school before, but never on such an extensive basis. Today's classroom teacher might have one or any combination of the following helpers available to work with her or him:

1. A professionally trained teacher's aide with training that might range from six weeks to two years.

2. An untrained aide hired by the school district to assist the teacher.

3. Preservice college interns, student teachers and other participators who work in schools from a few weeks at a time up to one full year or more.

4. Volunteer mothers and other volunteer lay individuals who donate their time and talent to the school.

5. Instructional television helpers who come into the classroom via the television set.

6. Other teachers who assume the helper role through teaming practices or through a special area talent or expertise that they represent.

7. Other professional people in the community such as doctors, lawyers, judges, etc., who share their professional experience with the school.

8. And even children fill the helper role through new programs where older children work with younger children or where a child has unique background in an area and agrees to share it with other teachers and children.

Yes, today's teacher finds a new dimension to his or her role in the function of coordinator and manager of a core of instructional helpers. It is most important that this role be taken very seriously as the task is challenging and many important questions relate to this area. For example, what

2. Laurence D. Haskew and Jonathon C. McLendon, *This is Teaching* (Glenview, Illinois: Scott, Foresman, 1968), p. 457.

tasks and roles can be performed by helpers who have not had any type of professional training? Does it matter as long as the person can perform satisfactorily in the teacher's professional judgment? What type of instructional decisions should "helpers" be able to make? How will this differ from one style or level of helper to another? Can and should children be exposed to larger numbers of teachers and helpers in the school environment? Does this vary depending upon the age of the child? Who should select the helpers? These represent only a small sampling of the questions the teacher must face in the helper world.

It is encouraging to have helpers available to the classroom teacher, and some valuable trade-offs look promising. Preservice teacher education students, for example, are highly motivated to work in real school environments as they work toward entering professional competencies. They have, in most instances, more professional training than the typically prepared teacher's aide and can offer the school district a rich resource of talent for their programs. On the one hand, the preservice teacher is gaining valuable on-site training with opportunities to work and interact with children, teachers, administrators, and community people making real decisions in concrete programs. By the same token the school districts reap benefits from the rich supply of young talent available to their on-going programs.

Teacher aides (trained or untrained) also offer much to the teacher. Several school districts have decided to hire, for example, four part-time teacher aides instead of filling one professional position they have open. They feel that having this team of aides available for use by the professional classroom teacher will reap greater benefits than an additional full-time staff member. These aides could then take on several of the responsibilities that generally require less professional preparation and allow the professional teacher time to concentrate on what are regarded to be more sophisticated instructional tasks. The aides serve basically as extensions of the classroom teacher with the professional teacher the key decision maker.

Mothers and fathers and other recruited resource individuals are also among the world of helpers a teacher has at her disposal—and a rich supply of resources they are. Here is an area where the school has generally fallen short in capitalizing on a natural rich resource of human beings to assist with a variety of school functions. A school as we have said earlier should really represent a social subsystem in itself which is subject to analysis by its membership. Since its most important element is people, there should be extensive opportunities provided children, teachers, and resource people to interact in meaningful ways on significant life problems and concerns natural to their environment and, in fact, there should be opportunities to examine and study that behavior. This might mean examining school management concerns together, i.e., students and teachers and not just teachers and administrators; it might mean cooperatively exploring and deciding upon new physical arrangements in the building, new arrangements on the playground or in the landscaping of the school property; it might mean responding as a community in some way to the human needs of one or more members of the school created by a fire, death, or some other tragedy; or it might mean just the opposite, responding as a community to some happy event that has occurred, a new baby in a family, an award received, an accomplishment of note, or any number of things.

The point is, the richer the mix of human beings the greater the potential. To illustrate how this portion of the teachers' helper world can meet a variety of needs simultaneously I offer this example. Primary teachers generally speaking feel a need for a more personalized approach to the teaching of reading. One single aspect of their concern is that children should have opportunities to read to someone and to have someone share in the excitement of the story. They try to stretch their instructional day so as to provide this opportunity to as many children as possible but, alas, they continue to fall far short of their goal. Here is an excellent chance for the helper to play a significant role. For example, what would be the possibilities of recruiting some of the elderly people in the community to assist with this most important instructional task? Could they not provide the school with some much needed 173 "ears" to listen and some "conversation" to talk briefly with a child about what he has read? I am not saying they should become the schools' reading instructors—I am only saying they might serve the listening role quite effectively. At the same time this need is being met, we might also have a few empty laps filled with children and have brought into the school environment a few additional portions of "patience"—a quality we don't have much of at any time. And what about the potential of seeing the world of the old interact with the world of the young? Are they separate worlds? Should they be? What ideas do you see to capitalize on this rich newly created mix of human beings?

The Legal World

Another rapidly growing world surrounding a teacher is the legal world. Today more than at any point in American educational history the public eye is critically examining the school setting and attempting to sort out its legal rights and responsibilities. Lawsuits which relate to physical punishment, academic freedom, child molesting, content of school programs, and other areas are becoming more common and frequent, and the impact on teachers is in some ways frightening.

Today's classroom teacher needs to be fully aware of the implications of these concerns and developments for his or her instructional practices. What constitutes "reasonable" supervision as it is referred to in school law literature and practice? What is the legal relationship of the local school to the state, and to the local community through the board of education? What laws and regulations guide the operation of schools?

Haskew and McLendon cite the four major sources of school law, namely:

1. State constitutions and legislation, embodying enactments based on the principle that state governments hold ultimate control over matters concerning schools.

2. State board of education regulations, promulgated to guide the operation of the state school systems.

3. Local school board regulations, dealing with many of the educational matters that state governments leave in the hands of local authorities.

4. Court decisions, involving the interpretation of stated policies and regulations or the application of common law to contested school cases. Most often it is a state court that rules on educational matters, though cases involving application of principles in the United States Constitution come under the jurisdiction of federal courts.[3]

It is within this framework that teachers will need to be knowledgeable for it affects much of the work in their classroom in addition to such matters as retirement plans, contract agreements, tenure, and a variety of related areas of concern.

A sound knowledge of the legal world surrounding teaching should serve for the most part as a supporting factor for the work of the teacher. There will be occasions, however, when teachers will have to guard against temptations to avoid certain instructional practices because they fear legal action. For example, it is easy to understand why a teacher hesitates to embrace a student in a school situation where affection seems natural—she is aware of lawsuits and actions that have been brought against other teachers for "touching" children. It is also easy to understand why many teachers avoid field trips and experiences and operate only from the "secure" framework of their classroom. Here again a sound knowledge of the world of law should make the teacher more secure in his or her day-to-day responsibilities.

The Professional World

A decision to become a teacher is a decision to join the largest professional group in the world. For example, there are over two million elementary and secondary teachers in the United States alone. If one were to tally all of the professional educators around the world, the total would be staggering, as the profession is made up of a wide variety of positions at all levels. Chandler, Powell, and Hazard offer a representative sampling of career opportunities in the field of education which clearly illustrate the variety:

I. Elementary schools—including nursery and kindergarten

    A. Classroom teacher

    B. Teacher of special subjects, such as music or art

3. From *This is Teaching* by Laurence D. Haskew and Jonathan C. McLendon. Copyright © by Scott, Foresman and Company. Reprinted by permission.

C. Teacher of subject in a departmentalized school
D. Teacher of exceptional children
E. Critic teacher in a laboratory school
F. Visiting teacher
G. Supervisor
H. Consultant
I. Director of research
J. Hearing therapist
K. Librarian
L. Speech correctionist
M. School psychologist
N. Assistant Principal
O. Principal

II. Secondary schools

A. Teacher of subject such as social studies or English
B. Department head
C. Guidance director
D. Athletic coach
E. Supervisor
F. Librarian
G. Visiting teacher
H. Consultant
I. Critic teacher in laboratory school
J. Assistant principal
K. Principal

III. Administrative and general services

A. Superintendent of schools
B. Assistant superintendent
C. Director of research
D. School psychologist
E. Attendance officer
F. Director, special fields such as public relations or audiovisual material
G. Vocational counselor

IV. College or university

A. Teacher
B. Critic teacher in laboratory school
C. Head of department
D. Principal of laboratory school
E. Dean of men
F. Dean of women
G. Business manager
H. Registrar

I. Director, special functions such as placement, public relations, and development
J. Dean of a college
K. Director of research
L. Assistant dean
M. Field worker in admissions
N. Alumni secretary
O. Vice President
P. President

V. State Departments of Education and U.S. Office of Education

A. Supervisor, special fields such as secondary education
B. Director of division
C. Assistant state superintendent
D. Superintendent of public instruction
E. Assistant commissioner of education
F. Commissioner of Education of the United States
G. Consultant to foreign governments

VI. Professional associations, such as state education associations and NEA

A. Field worker
B. Staff member
C. Research worker and writer
D. Director of division
E. Executive secretary

VII. Educational director or consultant to noneducational organizations

A. Business or industrial firms
B. Chambers of commerce
C. Service agencies, such as heart fund
D. Religious organizations
E. Director of recreation
F. Camping sponsored by various agencies
G. Youth groups—YMCA, YWCA
H. Instructor in a hospital
I. UNESCO
J. Boy and Girl Scouts
K. Labor organizations

VIII. Other opportunities

A. Free-lance writer
B. Member of educational consulting firm
C. Research worker
D. Employee of foundation
E. Teacher in adult education program

F. Free-lance lecturer

G. Teacher in church or Bible school[4]

To be part of such a large professional world carries with it both responsibilities and challenge. There are the responsibilities to maintain high professional standards in one's work in and out of the classroom. These standards are clearly outlined in adopted codes of ethics which apply at the national, state, and local levels. There is also the responsibility to the overall goals of the profession which include goals of social service and the autonomous decisions and behaviors which are usually left to the discretion of a professional group, in this case educators.

The organizational structures which make up the professional world are varied and diversified. The largest professional groups are the National Education Association and the American Federation of Teachers. Through these two major organizations teachers collectively strive for advancement of the teaching profession at all levels. Their overall goals are aimed in common directions, although the two are rivals in many ways. State and local associations are an integral part of the large network that comprises these two groups.

In addition to the organizations mentioned above, it is possible for educators to become a part of a number of other professional groups. For example, it is possible to join professional groups which relate to one's teaching field such as The National Council for Social Studies or similar organizations in math, English, etc. It is also possible to join professional groups where children become the focal point, as in the Association for Childhood Education. Professional groups without across-subject lines are also a possibility as in the case of the Association for Supervision and Curriculum Development. Then there are special area groups that exist such as the National Elementary Principals, American Association for Colleges of Teacher Education, Audio Visual Association, etc. If one were to list all of the professional associations and organizations at the international, national, state, and local levels several pages would be required. As a teacher you are or will likely be a member of four or five of these organizations at one time or another.

A teacher's professional world is also to be regarded as a rapidly changing world. Just within the last few years we have noted significant changes with regard to such matters as collective negotiations, teacher rights, administrator rights, and a host of other related areas of concern. The profession is just beginning to realize the power it has in numbers and the future will probably hold many other changes as it grows and develops. It will be important for teachers to keep societal goals and the role of the school in sharp perspective as they move the profession forward.

4. Reprinted by permission of Dodd, Mead & Company, Inc. from *Education and the New Teacher* by B. J. Chandler, Daniel Powell, and William R. Hazard. Copyright © 1971 by Dodd, Mead & Company, Inc.

The Community World

The community world also offers an additional dimension to the role of teacher. Teachers need to be aware of and knowledgeable about the communities in which they live. Perhaps even more important is their natural, active involvement in the life of the community. This involvement can and does take many shapes and forms. Community organizations, activism in the church, social interaction, civic affairs, and local policies are again only a sampling of the many possibilities.

For a number of years the teacher's involvement in the community was usually limited to career-related activities like Sunday school teaching, choir directing, scouting, etc. This is no longer true in most communities which are beginning to view the teacher as more of an integral part of all community life. As a teacher you will need to contribute, through your own behavior, to this common goal.

The World of the Future

Perhaps the most mystifying and challenging world of all that surrounds a teacher is the world of the future. What will it be like? What clues do we have? What will be the most significant experiences we can provide learners which will assist them in dealing adequately and comfortably with *tomorrow* as well as today? How far into the future should education and educators aim?

The questions are not new; in fact they are, I am sure, older than the very first graduation speech, which certainly must have offered a challenge to the graduates to reach out and mold the future in some significant way. At one time man perhaps was not staggered by the challenge to reach out and mold the future but today, with the greatly accelerated rate of change in our society, our minds are taxed beyond belief; what makes it more frustrating is our lack of knowledge and ability to cope with this challenge. As Toffler so aptly expresses it:

> Earnest intellectuals talk bravely about "educating for change" or "preparing people for the future." But we know virtually nothing about how to do it. In the most rapidly changing environment to which man has ever been exposed, we remain pitifully ignorant of how the human animal copes.[5]

As teachers we have little choice but to confront the future despite our lack of knowledge and sophistication about what it holds. Further we must do our very best to make today's experiences relevant for days to come. We need to seriously question much of what is going on in our schools today and maintain a continuous sorting process, to eliminate those aspects of our work with young people which are meaningless. New courses will need to be charted for coping with the rapidly changing society in which we live. We need to chart those courses free from the fear of failure, for any attempt to deal with the future is by its nature non-error free. As Toffler again states:

> In dealing with the future, at least for the purpose at hand, it is more important to be imaginative and insightful than to be one hundred percent "right." Theories do not have to be "right" to be enormously useful. Even error has its uses. The maps of the world drawn by the medieval cartographers were so hopelessly inaccurate, so filled with factual error, that they elicit condescending smiles today when almost the entire surface of the earth has been charted. Yet the great explorers could never have discovered the New World without them. Nor could the better, more accurate maps of today have been drawn until men, working with the limited evidence available to them, set down on paper their bold conceptions of worlds they had never seen.[6]

You are the mapmaker of the future so chart your course carefully, but most importantly *chart it.*

5. Alvin Toffler, *Future Shock* (New York: Random House, 1970), pp. 2-3.
6. Ibid., p. 6.

There are many other worlds that we might have visited: the world of evaluation, the world of ideas, the world of organization, the international world, and of course many more. You will need to sort out and explore these many worlds in your role as teacher. From one teacher to another, I understand the weight of the challenge. May your trip be enjoyable.

QUESTIONS FOR ANALYSIS

1. What problems do you see in the helper world referred to in this chapter? Is it natural for all of these people to get along together? If not, what can you do to contribute to the best relations possible?

2. What do you consider to be the most serious challenge facing educators in the future?

3. What other worlds would you add to those that were mentioned in this chapter?

4. How will you, or do you, use technology in your work with children in the classroom?

5. Has technology been misused in any way in the world of education?

6. What potential do you see in having older students work with younger students in your world of helpers? What are the values as well as potential dangers?

7. Describe your background in the area of school law. If limited, how can you acquire more knowledge and insight?

8. What do you consider to be the most serious issues surrounding the collective negotiation movement which has developed in recent years in the education profession?

SELECTED REFERENCES

Anderson, Robert H. *Teaching in a World of Change.* New York: Harcourt Brace Jovanovich, 1966.

Avila, Donald L.; Combs, Arthur W.; Purkey, William W. *The Helping Relationship Sourcebook.* Boston: Allyn and Bacon, 1971.

Chandler B. J.; Powell, Daniel; Hazard, William R. *Education and the New Teacher.* New York: Dodd, Mead, 1971.

Combs, Arthur W. *The Professional Education of Teachers.* Boston: Allyn and Bacon, 1965.

Combs, Arthur W.; Avila, Donald L.; Purkey, William W. *Helping Relationships: Basic Concepts for the Helping Professions.* Boston: Allyn and Bacon, 1971.

Denemark, George W. "The Teacher and His Staff." *N.E.A. Journal,* December 1966.

Glasser, William, M.D. *Schools without Failure.* New York: Harper and Row, Publishers, 1969.

Haskew, Laurence D., and McLendon, Jonathon C. *This is Teaching.* Glenview, Illinois: Scott, Foresman, 1968.

Muller, Herbert J. *The Children of Frankenstein.* Bloomington, Indiana: Indiana University Press, 1971.

Silberman, Charles E. *Crisis in the Classroom.* New York: Random House, 1970.

Toffler, Alvin. *Future Shock.* New York: Random House, 1970.

182

THE
TEACHER:
Rewards

Teachers come in many sizes and shapes—large, small, young, old, tired, fresh, black, white, rich, poor.

Some are kind, and some are not.

Those who are mean are stinky.

Some teachers know how to make you feel good;

Others make you feel bad all over, deep down.

Some help you not be afraid;

Others keep you scared all the time;

Some show you what you might try;

Others tell you that you can't do it.

They are No-No teachers. They're stinky.

Lots of teachers go to college after they finish teaching you to see if they can learn some more.

Some learn; some don't. Some it helps; some it don't.

Those who don't try to learn and understand are stinky.

Some teachers make you want to come to school every day;

Some teachers make you want to skip out as often as you can.

I've had two who made me wish I had school on Saturday.

I've been lucky. Some kids never find teachers like that.

Some bring you lots of things to work with;

Others make you stay in your seat and fill in blanks and memorize stuff.

Those teachers are stinky.

They say stinky words, give you stinky looks, and grade you on stinky report cards.

Some teachers are great. Like I said, I had two like that.

They put bandage on my hurts—on my heart, on my mind, on my spirit.

Those teachers cared about me and let me know it.

They gave me wings.[1]

As the thoughts of a dropout illustrate, teachers come in many sizes and shapes and represent a wide variety of impacts on learners. As has been pointed out throughout the analysis we have among our ranks great, good, average, and some unbelievably bad teachers who clearly don't belong. Most of us would like to be one of the two great teachers our dropout talks about; such teachers provide "wings," the meaningful experiences for mind, heart, and spirit—but it is not easy to earn such compliments. Again as we have explored earlier, to be great means to sacrifice in many ways, to be willing to serve in many capacities—as an active agent of change in an institution undergoing dramatic and dynamic reevaluation; as an individual, who shares freely and openly your own strengths and weaknesses as you explore side by side with youth and significant issues of our times. This kind of service means that you spend time (lots of it) interacting with all styles of people, genuinely interested in their problems as related to areas you are exploring with them; it means that you are not able to leave your work completely behind you when you walk out of the school, for the school is only a point of departure for your people-centered work; it means that you are willing to live comfortably with a range of emo-

1. Marian Franklin, "Thoughts of a Dropout." *Today's Education: NEA Journal*, February, 1970.

tions which take you from psychological highs in terms of the joy and happiness that surrounds much of what you should do in the school environment to unbelievably low feelings which surround various situations; it means that you give time and devoted effort toward maintaining high levels of scholarship in the areas of your work; it means that you are willing and able to deal with the many tensions and pressures that surround education and a host of other areas which make the world of teaching challenging, tough, and exhausting. But for those who are willing and able *it is worth it—for the rewards are many.*

Person-to-Person Rewards

It is difficult to describe the tremendous satisfaction that comes from helping another human being and responding to his or her needs. To know that you have really helped someone and to receive that individual's gratitude builds self-adequacy in a powerful way; it fulfills one of our most significant needs—to live comfortably with ourselves. The rewards take many forms. A five-year-old grabs your hand and leads you to an area where he can share an accomplishment with you or ask for help. As you sit with him, he unlocks the mysteries of our printed language which hold some information he needs, and he says, "Mr. Johnson, isn't this exciting? I didn't know that before." And then again he may simply share a smile or some other nonverbal human exchange with you which says that all is well with the world and that the relationship between child and teacher is comfortable as they go about the important work of the day.

The rewards are much the same in learning environments involving older children or adults. Perhaps the language is a bit more sophisticated but the feelings that surround a job well done are what really count. There is no way possible of simulating the feeling because of its personal nature, but put yourself in front of a warm smile or a comment like: "I can't tell you how much I have enjoyed being in your class. I learned so much and you made me feel so comfortable with myself and others. You really cared about each of us and we are all grateful for your hard work." Of course, the comment is hollow without a real person behind it and a real person receiving it. But these situations do exist for good teachers and within them lies the real reward of being a teacher.

Observing Growth in Others

Direct person-to-person feedback is not the only source of such rewards. Sometimes one simply observes the growth of an individual or individuals in reading ability, in refining skills in mathematics, in communicating or interacting with others, in becoming more self-confident, or in any area for that matter. It might come by way of having knowledge of the success your students enjoy after they have left your classroom. It is indeed rewarding to observe and to be an influencing part of the growth and development of any human being. As a television commercial expresses it: *Try it, you'll like it.*

A Sharing Outlet

There are many other rewarding dimensions to the role of teacher. Having the opportunity to deal with a wide range of individuals as I have already pointed out is, to say the least, challenging and very difficult. But it is also rewarding in that it provides opportunities for mutual sharing of respect, love, trust, encouragement, understanding and other valued aspects of life and living. And what good are these unless they can be shared? The rich mix of human beings that are part of the world of education provides many opportunities for sharing. The teacher of course needs to translate these opportunities into meaningful behavior.

Social Activism Rewards

Those who feel a need for social activism will, or at least should, find an additional source of reward in teaching. In a live and vibrant school environment, teachers and students alike should be touching down on and dealing with many real world concerns and issues. It might mean dealing with a local pollution problem, an election or a local drug problem. It might mean dealing with national concerns like war, race relations, or federal aid to education. Whatever the concern the point is that teachers and students should assume more than passive roles in examining the issue and as a result become active agents of change in our society. This is rewarding for both the teacher and the student.

The Reward of Growth

Almost everyone has a built-in desire to grow and develop to his or her fullest capacity. Teaching provides an excellent arena where such growth should occur quite naturally because of the teacher's role. As we have illustrated several times throughout this analysis the teacher is not a ready-made storehouse and disseminater of knowledge. On the contrary a teacher must continue to learn and grow with the students and it is this growing edge that provides many satisfactions and rewards. The reward may come through probing more deeply into one's field of study in a quest of new data to assist with a problem-solving endeavor; it may come through a detailed study of a community problem with students; it could come through formal or informal contact with teaching colleagues who are exploring other areas of concern to them and their classes; it may come through a teacher's personal growth and development style in continuing education (workshops, college experiences, travel, professional reading, etc.); or it may come as a result of the day-to-day contact teachers have with a great variety of human beings and the associations with them. For example, much will be learned from the children you work with as they assume the role of teacher on a number of occasions.

187

Whatever the source, and there are many more, the teacher is in an excellent position to be stimulated to grow and develop personally and professionally in many ways. Again, it doesn't happen automatically but the stimulus in and of itself should set the stage for many satisfying areas of growth and rewards for the teacher who capitalizes on the opportunities. Teaching demands continuous growth.

The Rewards of Recognition and Acceptance

Although the potential reward of recognition and acceptance in teaching has been debated down through the years, it is my feeling that teachers do enjoy great satisfactions with social recognition and acceptance. Even though the teaching profession is coming under a more direct evaluation by the public (which I believe is healthy), it still is ranked in the upper third of all vocations and I have no reason to believe that this will not continue to be the case in the years ahead. Teachers have a tendency to depreciate their image in the communities they serve and I am not convinced this is an accurate perception on their part. From what I have observed teachers are generally looked up to in a community, admired (perhaps more than is

desirable) for having a wide range of knowledge, respected for the educational backgrounds they possess, and admired and respected for the important positions they occupy in working with today's youth.

It would be presumptuous of course to pretend that no problems exist. For example, many families in the high socioeconomic brackets in a community "role play" a relationship with teachers, which appears to be full of respect and admiration for teachers, but when it comes right down to real decisions in country clubs, social gatherings, and major community activities their behavior clearly indicates that the teacher is not cut from the appropriate piece of fabric to "fit in." But this represents only one area and generally speaking a very small segment of any community. This leads me to another debatable reward—money.

Financial Rewards

It appears to be a fact that very few teachers get rich in the total societal frame of reference. They generally don't own large homes, yachts, or have swimming pools and tennis courts in their backyards. They generally don't travel abroad at will or vacation at major vacation centers throughout the world as is true of individuals whose incomes greatly surpass the average teacher's salary. But teachers are far from being "poor" in the total societal sense and generally enjoy a very secure economic base in their lives. This is not to say that teachers are earning enough for their professional efforts—they are not. Higher salaries are needed for such an important professional activity as teaching and along with higher salaries must come some dramatic changes in the style of work teachers do. I believe we must be held accountable for our efforts.

I am saying, therefore, that there is a financial reward in teaching if you are willing to examine the broader frame of reference of man and his financial relationship to his world. Buying power, working conditions, fringe benefits, personal property gains, mobility, and a number of other economic factors place teachers well ahead of many human beings around the world. Perhaps people in general should broaden their interpretation of "richness" to include more than money. Whenever that occurs, teachers will be among the richest people in the world. It is the only type of richness that seems to make sense and I am alarmed and troubled with man's difficulty in being comfortable with it. Man's relationship with himself, others, and his world can be comfortable in a variety of occupations if the work is the goal, not "economic accumulations." Think about it before you decide to be a teacher and, if you are a teacher, *remember it.*

Yes, the potential rewards in teaching are many and for those who are willing to sacrifice and commit themselves to the most challenging profession I know, a rich life awaits. But it will not come easy and you must be prepared to share the pains and frustrations as well, for it is only within that total framework where your mind, heart, and spirit will echo the feeling— *it's great to be a teacher*—and it really is.   189

QUESTIONS FOR ANALYSIS

1. What rewards, other than those identified in this chapter, do you experience or foresee in a career in classroom teaching?

2. If you had to identify one single reward that would stand above all others in classroom teaching, what would it be? What are the reasons for your choice?

3. How can you personally make life more rewarding for the teachers, administrators, and children with whom you work, or with whom you will work, in schools?

4. What are your personal thoughts on financial rewards and classroom teaching?

SELECTED REFERENCES

Dennison, George. *The Lives of Children.* New York: Random House, 1969.

Greenberg, Herbert M. *Teaching with Feeling.* New York: Pegasus, 1969.

Jersild, Arthur T. *When Teachers Face Themselves.* New York: Teachers College, Columbia University, 1955.

Ryan, Kevin, and Cooper, James M. *Kaleidoscope: Readings in Education.* Boston: Houghton Mifflin, 1972.

Ryan, Kevin, and Cooper, James M. *Those Who Can, Teach.* Boston: Houghton Mifflin, 1972.

NOTES

THE
TEACHER:
Your Concept?

The search for meaning is not a search for an abstract body of knowledge,
or even for a concrete body of knowledge. It is a distinctly personal
search. The one who makes it raises intimate personal questions: What
really counts, for me? What values am I seeking? What, in my existence
as a person, in my relations with others, in my work as a teacher,
is of real concern to me, perhaps of ultimate concern to me? In my
teaching I seek to transmit the meanings others have found in their search
for truth, and that is good as far as it goes. But as I try to help young
people to discover meaning, have I perhaps evaded the question of what
life might mean to me? How can I, in my study and my teaching and in the
countless topics that engage my thought, find a home within myself?[1]

1. Reprinted by permission of the publisher from Arthur T. Jersild,
When Teachers Face Themselves. (New York: Teachers College Press,
1969; Copyright 1955 by Teachers College, Columbia University), pp.
4-5.

What has been shared in the preceding chapters is my concept of teacher. It is only one of many concepts that exist. It is personal and honest; it represents the frame of reference that I, as an individual, use to bring meaning to my quest for a better understanding of my role as teacher.

I have not offered my concept of teacher with the idea of selling it to others. I did not acquire my concept in that fashion nor do I feel it is even possible to take on, by way of the printed word, the basic set of beliefs that holds such a complex concept together. On the contrary I recognize that reading about the beliefs of others is only one of a variety of experiences and encounters that contribute to an individual's concept of what a teacher should be. Therefore, I only offer my concept of teacher as stimulus for thought as you go about the most important activity of all—*framing and refining your concept of teacher.* How does it read?